God Knows
Grandparents
Make a
Difference

God Knows Caregiving Can Pull You Apart:
12 Ways to Keep It All Together

God Knows Parenting Is a Wild Ride:
9 Things to Hold on To

God Knows Marriage Isn't Always Easy:
12 Ways to Add Zest

God Knows We Get Angry:
Healthy Ways to Deal With It

God Knows You're Stressed:
Simple Ways to Restore Your Balance

God Knows You're Grieving:
Things to Do to Help You Through

God Knows You'd Like a New Body:
12 Ways to Befriend the One You've Got

God Knows
Grandparents
Make a
Difference

Ways to share your wisdom

Priscilla J. Herbison
Cynthia Herbison Tambornino

 SORIN BOOKS   Notre Dame, IN

As publisher of the *GOD KNOWS* series, SORIN BOOKS is dedicated to providing resources to assist readers to enhance their quality of life. We welcome your comments and suggestions, which may be conveyed to:

SORIN BOOKS
P.O. BOX 1006
Notre Dame, IN 46556-1006
Fax: 1-800-282-5681
e-mail: sorinbk@nd.edu

www.sorinbooks.com

International Standard Book Number: 1-893732-50-9

Cover and text design by Katherine Robinson Coleman

Printed and bound in the United States of America.

Library of Congress Cataloging-in-Publication Data
Herbison, Priscilla J.
   God knows grandparents make a difference : ways to share your wisdom /
Priscilla J. Herbison, Cynthia M. Tambornino.
      p. cm. -- (God knows)
   ISBN 1-893732-50-9
   1. Grandparents--Religious life. I. Tambornino, Cynthia M. II. Title.
III. Series.
   BV4528.5 .H47 2003
   248.8'45--dc21
                                                    2002014555
                                                    CIP

CONTENTS

Introduction

If you are a new grandparent or one who has a flock of grandchildren, you will know or know already that grandparenting is at once joyful and saddening, invigorating and exhausting, funny and sobering, mostly filled with love, but sometimes touched by anger and fear. In any case, even though some folks that we know were reluctant grandparents, none—as their stories will show—have found the experience one that they would trade for all the treasures in the world.

Nobel Prize winner Elie Weisel relates a Jewish saying that the Holy One created humans because God loves stories. And we humans emulate God in our love of stories. We love stories because they tell us who we are. Stories make us feel less alone. They connect generations, entertain, and reveal the holy. It could be that is what the writer Joan Didion was touching on when she said we tell stories to live.

Along the way, as we have gathered our stories, we've found that all of these reasons are fulfilled. And we've learned. We've found that not only are grandchildren gifts, but we are gifts to them, which we sometimes forget in the joy of grandparenting.

Other lessons stand out:

- A grandparent's love is probably the most pure and powerful love because it is so unconditional.

- The grandparent-grandchild relationship is a love story.

- Increasingly, because of the challenges of our times, grandparents are becoming parents again. You may be among the estimated seven million grandparents who are rearing their grandchildren at least on a part-time basis.

- The love of a grandchild with special needs can give us a foretaste of heaven. They teach us what life and love are all about.

- Part of the freedom in grandparenting comes from how close we are in nature, in learning styles, and interests to our grandchildren. There's something true about traits skipping generations. We're reminded of the Egyptian saying, "Nearer than our children are the children of our children."

- We now have the time and the calm to just watch our grandchildren grow.

- We're just nuts about our grandchildren and can enjoy everything they do and say. And we can enjoy being a teacher of these little ones as we step back and draw connections between generations.

- We're old enough and experienced enough to look at one another and share the joys and sorrows, ups and downs that we all experience. We are freer than we were when we raised our children. We talk more candidly and are more open with each other than we ever were before. Grandparents are more tolerant. As parents we may have been burdened with guilt over some of the behavior of our children. From the position of a grandparent, we can see not only our children, but also our grandchildren's future, and we can assure them that all will be well.

- Grandparenting and acquiring wisdom is a story of dynamic growth. It's not a static thing to be achieved. We continue to grow in the relationship. Sometimes the grandchild teaches us how to grow. Sometimes we can learn from our grandchildren.

Next to unconditional love, wisdom is the gift most cherished by grandchildren. What is wisdom but the life and breath of the sacred Spirit within us? Even more than that, when we thought about the cherished legacy of grandparents, it struck us that the qualities of wisdom are listed in one of our favorite readings from Paul's letter to the Galatians (5:22-23) in the Bible: love, joy, peace, patience, kindness, generosity, goodness, faithfulness, gentleness, humility, and self-control.

What do these fruits of wisdom look like? How do we nurture and cultivate these fruits so our grandchildren can taste and savor them? The stories that we've collected illustrate this wisdom in action. In *The Shape of Living*, David Ford writes:

> Because wisdom is so much a matter of making the deep connections in the midst of the complexities of life, there is no substitute for seeing how someone does it. But, more than just seeing, it is a matter of being seen. The wise see in us our potential. They listen to us with the "inner ear." They open us up, inspire us, energize us, and allow us to blossom, and give us the sense that there is always more. Excellence is the aim, yet they are patient with us. It is a gentle, utterly respectful overwhelming, at the heart of which is delight in truth and goodness. The classic sign of this is immense gratitude, increasing as wisdom is tested and developed, together with the desire to pass it on. (p. 95)

The Fruits of Grandparent Wisdom

As grandparents, we are in a privileged position to be channels of the fruits of wisdom for our grandchildren, as Cynthia vividly experienced on a glorious day in early June.

Cameron Alexander, her fourteenth grandchild, was born the evening before. As Cynthia took three of her granddaughters to a nearby playground so their mothers could visit their sister and new nephew in the hospital, she reflected about her week.

Her odometer told her what she already knew. She had put over 200 miles on her car driving to one grandchild's dance recital, another's choral concert, and a trio of grandchildren's chamber ensemble performances. Then from the back seat of her car came the angelic sound of her three youngest granddaughter's voices. They were singing, perfectly on key, their pure light voices following the lead of a flute in a Mozart symphony.

Cynthia thought of well-meaning, but discouraging, advice passed on to her and to her children: in effect, that music should only be an avocation, a hobby, and not a vocation. She remembered Priscilla telling her a true story about a grandmother who called her grandson to her deathbed for her last words. The old woman lifted her head off her pillow, looked her grandson in the eye and said these parting words, "Don't ever become a musician!"

Despite that advice, Cynthia had encouraged her children's love of music, and now would support her grandchildren in their love of music. For she had known herself of the joy and peace the gift of music had been for her and of the love she could give to others through music. She remembered a priest-musician once saying, "If music is the voice of God, musicians are blessed to be his instruments to bring joy to all the earth."

And so, Cynthia would say to her grandchildren, as she had said to her children, that if they had a burning desire to pursue the love of this gift of music that they had been given, to by all means follow it as their vocation. And if they needed to support themselves by other means, cultivate music anyway because if they didn't express their God-given gift, they would likely find themselves blocked in other areas of life.

"You won't feel complete," Cynthia said to her children and now her grandchildren. "You can volunteer to sing or perform, or you can encourage the gift in your own and other's children. And you can give yourself the gift of joy. It's impossible to sing and be depressed at the same time!" So the gift of music goes on in endless song, even to the next generation.

Cynthia recalled her thoughts as she watched her granddaughter listen and frolic in the audience during a concert Cynthia was directing some time ago:

> I watch her in the audience as she listens intently to the voices of my chorus. Her blonde curls bounce up and down each time she goes from her chair to her daddy's lap and back to her chair again. The family's tapestry is woven of one golden thread weaving through each generation, tying together the commonality passed down from grandmother to granddaughters, from grandfathers to grandsons. I think this as I see my eldest granddaughter sitting in enjoyment at my concert. Only yesterday, it seems she was a small girl without a care in the world, running through my front door heading straight for the piano in my living room. That legacy—my passion for music—has been passed down to her generation, and it puts a song in my heart that will play forever.

The wisdom and strength of grandparent love does carry on. It is powerful.

Using the Book

The stories and remarks, reflections and quotes in this book come from our experience and the wisdom of experts, friends, and family. Our words and stories are meant to encourage your own reflection about the joys and sorrows, challenges and privileges of grandparenting. We invite you to discover your own grandparent-wisdom.

The exercises and quotations we have selected will help you cultivate and process your love for your grandchildren, legacies of wisdom, courage, and generosity. Finally, we hope you will find ideas to support and encourage you as you care for your grandchildren and prepare them for leadership in this new millennium.

Special Thanks

No work of art or writing is ever accomplished without the invaluable and usable support of others. We want to thank our editor, Carl Koch, without whose robust encouragement and matchless skill this book would never have been written. Thanks also to Carole Gesme and the First Friday Group (you know who you are) for your stories. Finally, special thanks to Sharon Votel for her quotes and everlasting support.

The stories in this book are true. Stories with no author ascribed were written by people who wanted their names withheld or by the two of us. With two exceptions, we have changed the identities of the characters so that any resemblance to anyone living or dead is purely coincidental.

We give special thanks to the courageous grandparents, whose names will remain anonymous, who are rearing their grandchildren. Their example uplifts all of us.

Be Blessed

Renowned psychologist and teacher Erich Fromm once remarked that "Birth is not one act; it is a process. The aim of life is to be fully born, though its tragedy is that most of us die before we are thus born. To live is to be born every minute."

Our hope for you is that grandparenting will be not only a celebration of the new life of your grandchildren, but a rebirth for you also. We ask that you be blessed by being born to new wisdom, fresh visions of the future, and new convictions about the grandeur of living.

1

Face It, You're in Love Again

GRANDCHILDREN ARE THE LOVE
AFFAIR OF OLD AGE.

Anne Morrow Lindbergh

If you want to get an idea of what God's unconditional love looks like, ask any grandparent. At a conference attended by more than five hundred people at St.
Olaf Church in Minneapolis, Reverend Thomas
Keating asked, "How many of you are grandparents?"
Over half raised their hands. "Do you remember how
you felt the first time your grandson or granddaughter
actually gazed at you and smiled in recognition?" A
warm wave of laughter rippled through the church.

"I've noticed," Keating continued, "that when that
grandchild first smiles and recognizes his grandmother
or granddad, that grandparent is in ecstasy for weeks
on end. Why, their feet hardly touch the ground! And
what does that little infant do to draw such a response?
Nothing! He just is! And for the grandparent, his smile
is the sun, the stars, and the moon all wrapped up.
That's what God's love is for us, and all we have to do
is be."

According to our friend Mary White, Keating got it
right. When she realized her first grandchild was going

to be born any day, Mary said, "I couldn't sleep. I'd wake up in the middle of the night with the moonlight streaming in, and I'd shiver in anticipation, wondering what he or she would look like and when she or he was coming. The daytime wasn't much different. Every time the phone rang I'd run trembling, hoping the call would be from my son-in-law telling me they were on their way to the hospital. The only other time I ever felt like that was when I fell in love. It's the only thing I can compare it to."

Our friend Marie Merrigan agrees: "I was just unprepared for the rush of feeling I had when I held my grandchild in my arms for the first time. The intensity of love was powerful."

Dr. Joe Tambornino, himself the father of eight surviving children, agreed. "Every time I see those babies, the feeling is so strong. It's as though I fall overboard with love." Moreover, if a grandparent can be in the delivery room when grandchildren are first born, hold them just for a minute, sense the dew smell and their soft tender skin, the experience is miraculous. Grandparents feel that it's important to be there, especially since the fathers were often kept out of the delivery room when they had their children or because they—as mothers—were knocked out with anesthetic when their own children were born. To behold that first gaze of recognition makes a magical moment.

As a photographer, Priscilla had the privilege of witnessing that gaze of recognition that passes between a newborn and his grandmother. She was asked to photograph her nephew Joe and his wife Caramia's first child. Their posture was, like many new parents, straight-backed with pride and more than a little cautious as though they might drop the baby. The baby's gaze was serene. When the infant was presented to his great-grandmother, Priscilla's mother whom the children all called Grannini or Gran, a dramatic change came over the baby's face. Grannini's frail arms suddenly grew as strong as willow branches. The cradle she made with her arms held him gently and securely. And at the sound of her soft voice murmuring endearments, he opened his eyes wide. The look of recognition on the baby's face seemed to say, "I know you!" And then he smiled and began to coo in response. At that moment, the words of a George McDonald poem came to mind: "Where did you come from baby dear / Out of the nowhere into the here." Into a circle of love.

Even with all the knowledge they have acquired over the years of the potential for sadness and loss, grandparents bring to their grandchildren fresh love and hope that enlivens them and forms a golden thread for the future.

GRANDPARENTS ARE FOR UNCONDI-

TIONAL LOVE—MEANT TO EXPRESS

THE EXTRAORDINARY AND WONDER-

FUL BELIEF THAT THERE NEVER WERE

ANY CHILDREN AS ADORABLE, BRIL-

LIANT, AND BEAUTIFUL AS THEIR OWN

GRANDCHILDREN.

Eda LeShan

Face It, You're in Love Again

- Collect poems or songs to sing or read to your new-born grandchild; make a sampler or calligraphy of a nursery rhyme to give to your grandchild.

- Remember a time when your own grandparent somewhere, sometime thought that you did some-thing beautiful or perfectly. How did that make you feel inside?

- Imagine that you are held in the arms of your grandparent. Let the worries, cares, and disappointments, anger and sorrow, and loneliness slip away. You are surrounded by love. You are secure in the warmth of their smile.

A GRANDPARENT ARRIVES THREE HOURS EARLY FOR YOUR BAPTISM, YOUR GRADUATION AND YOUR WEDDING BECAUSE HE OR SHE WANTS A SEAT WHERE HE OR SHE CAN SEE EVERYTHING.

Erma Bombeck

Grandson Number One

Being at the birth of my first grandchild, Adam, was my daughter-in-law's precious gift to me. I wasn't able to have children biologically, so we adopted our children. Kathy, my son Tad's wife, had been estranged from her mother for a myriad of logical reasons. So when Kathy and Tad announced they were going to have a baby and give us our first grandchild in January, I was ecstatic. Kathy and I were close, but the pregnancy drew us closer, especially since Tad had to be on the road so much during those first six months.

I accompanied Kathy to her doctor's office and she and I watched in awe when the ultrasound scans showed the baby's full form, sucking his thumb. I even went to some maternity classes with Kathy. But my son began to resent my closeness to Kathy, perhaps jealous that he hadn't been able to be in on these special moments.

Just before Christmas, Tad called and said, "Mom,
I don't want to hurt your feelings, but I've decided I
really just want to be with Kathy alone when she
delivers. Anyway, I don't think the doctors want all
kinds of people around getting in the way either.
Okay, Mom?"

I was hurt. Kathy had told me more than once that
she wanted me in the labor room because I had missed
out on the experience. It was her gift to me. But I swallowed my pain and heard myself saying, "Sure, I
understand. Just let me know how and when you and
Kathy would like us there and [I swallowed the lump
in my throat] how I can best help out."

"Thanks, Mom," he said. "We'll see you on
Christmas Day!"

I'll never forget the day Kathy went into labor. It
was mid-January in 1991. President Bush ordered
Army Reserve units into Desert Storm, and Minnesota
was locked into the grip of an ice storm. Everything
was covered with a sheath of ice. No travel was
advised. Some communities were without power. At
three in the morning the phone rang. It was Tad.

"Mom," he said. I could hear the anxiety in his
voice. "Kathy's having a really hard time, and she's crying for you. She needs you to rub her back. She says
you've got the touch. Can you come right away?"

"I'm on my way," I said, fully awake, my feet hit-
ting the floor.

"And, Mom," Tad pleaded, "could you stop and
pick up a bacon double cheeseburger. There's no food
except in vending machines, and I'm starving!"

"Where are you going?" my husband, still half-
asleep, said from the other side of the bed.

"To the hospital. Kathy needs me."

"You're not going out in that storm!"

"Watch me," I snapped.

By now, he was rolling out of bed. Pulling his chinos
over his pajama bottoms, a sweatshirt over his pajama

top, he padded down the stairs after me. He stuffed his bare feet into his Sorrel Boots.

Somehow, by the grace of God, we first slid our way to a fast-food restaurant for the bacon double cheese-burger, french fries, and coffee—enough for the whole maternity ward—then to the hospital. The roads were so bad that traffic was nonexistent. We made the trip in twenty-four minutes flat.

Kathy was a wreck. My husband took Tad out of the room for a moment on the pretense of getting him fed. I helped Kathy get into a more comfortable position so she was semi-upright and her pelvis was free to circle or rock. I positioned pillows at her back for support. After I refreshed her forehead and neck with a cool compress, I asked her if she wanted me to massage her back.

"Yes, that's what I really need." I massaged her shoulders and feet with firm, slow strokes and felt the tension ease. I told her how well she was doing.

Kathy's labor went very quickly after that. Tad and my husband joined us. And a wonderful surprise, my best friend Dana, a pediatrician, happened to be on call that night. So she joined us just as the baby's head crowned.

Kathy wept joyfully as Adam was placed on her chest. Tad caressed her check and then the baby's. I felt Kathy's hand clasp mine. Tad and Kathy drew me toward them and let my arms circle the baby.

Suddenly all was in motion. The baby was being weighed. Dana was checking Adam's fingers and toes. He was cleaned and swaddled in double blankets and passed to Tad. Tad looked at me shyly, came over, and placed him in my arms.

Others have tried to tell me what this moment is like, but I was unprepared for the rush of love I felt when he looked at me with those deep violet eyes. Babies aren't supposed to fix a gaze that early, but I swear he looked right back at me. With the sensuousness of the smell of his soft skin, I was transported.

While I love all my grandchildren deeply, there is a special connection with Adam. We are so alike in the way we solve problems and how we look at the world. I will always be grateful to Kathy for the priceless gift of being with her in labor—in her primitive pain and in the ecstasy of giving birth.

"LITTLE DID I REALIZE WHEN WE STOOD BEFORE THE MINISTER," SAID THE SILVER-HAIRED MAN, "THAT FORTY YEARS LATER, AND WITHOUT ANY TEETH, I'D BE EATING PEANUT BRITTLE TO KEEP FROM HURTING THE FEELINGS OF A TWELVE-YEAR-OLD GRANDDAUGHTER WHOSE SCOUT TROOP IS SELLING THE STUFF."

Anonymous

Matriarch-Grandmother

Sylvia Little has seven grandchildren and fourteen great-grandchildren. She is the matriarch of her family. Last week she went over to her granddaughter's house to deliver her four-year-old great-grandchild's birthday gift a day early. They played through the afternoon, had supper, and the day ended blissfully.

Sylvia had singing engagements the day of the child's birthday. Besides, she knew her great-grandchild would be having a lavish party—the guest list of which included all her little friends, brothers and sisters, aunts and uncles, and grandparents.

As Sylvia opened the door to her house, she could hear her phone ringing. She answered it. It was the trembling voice of her great-grandchild. "Grandma, where were you today? Didn't you know it was my birthday?"

"Well, honey," Sylvia said, a little surprised, "I came over yesterday and thought we had a grand time, just the two of us. Don't you remember? I brought your present over yesterday!"

"But, Grandma, today is my birthday and I waited for you all day. It's you I want, not the present!"

PERFECT LOVE SOMETIMES DOES
NOT COME UNTIL GRANDCHILDREN
ARE BORN.

Welsh Proverb

2

Rejoice in the Freedom of Grandparenting

It's nice being a grandchild. You're sitting on the floor being screamed at by Mommy for shaving the oriental rug with Daddy's razor, and the phone rings, and it's Granddaddy saying, "Bring that kid over here so I can love him up!"

Russell Baker

One recent spring in a public school fifth-grade classroom, a teacher was about to dole out punishment to the entire class as a reaction to the disruptive behavior of three students. She paused after describing how they would all have to pay for the behavior of a few when one of the students in the fourth row spoke up, "Miss Ellen, do you know who my grandfather is?"

Miss Ellen did indeed know of the student's grandfather. Keith Cross was superintendent of schools when she was first hired. Keith, the kid's grandfather, was renowned for his fairness, vision, and wisdom. Even though he was retired, his opinion was the one that lawmakers, current superintendents, and journalists sought, especially in a crisis. Without skipping a beat, Miss Ellen said, "We will let it pass. This time."

It didn't take long for the story of this incident to make its way to the teacher's lounge. "You know, El," Mark Smith, the eighth-grade teacher said, "you could discipline Keith's own kids, all seven of them, when they were here. But don't you dare even think about it with one of Keith's grandkids. You'll rue the day. He absolutely dotes on those grandchildren."

Another teacher, Larry Brown, added, "I remember how Keith never, I mean never, closed the schools because of snow or ice. Old Jerry Jones thought he could get to the father by going through Keith's son, Robbie. So, one morning after a seven-inch snowfall, Jones went up to Robbie and said, 'Why is it that your dad will never close the schools when we have a near blizzard outside?' Robbie looked Jones straight in the eye and said, 'You'll have to take that up with my dad. Anyway, Dad would have to answer to my mom, 'cause if he closed the schools, she'd have to stay home with all of us cooped up in the house all day.'

"Yeah," continued Larry, "Keith was tough, but fair. He'd never ask us to do what he wouldn't do. But with his grandkids, now that's another story! I've seen him deliver the grandkids to the school in the winter and pick them up and carry them over snow banks to the school's front door after a heavy snow."

Grandparenting can definitely be freeing. As a grandparent, we can be relaxed and enjoy our grand-children in a way that wasn't possible when we were a parent. We now have the leisure time and perspective to simply enjoy and love them just as they are. As parents we had the burden of childcare at all hours of the day and night, discipline, and making a decent living for our family.

Our worries were multiple: Were we too strict or too lenient in discipline? Were our children being carefully educated in school? When our children were infants, we could be worn to a frazzle with night feedings, childhood illness, and overnight changes in temperament—all of this while needing to be up for work the next day.

Our experience rearing our own children and our honesty give us the added advantage of perspective and discernment. One of my grandmother friends illustrated this for me. Just the other day, she told me, she took her five-year-old grandson to a science museum. As she drove along a busy interstate that would take them from their quiet neighborhood to the museum in the city, she noticed her grandson gazing thoughtfully out the window. Reflecting about when she was raising her own kids, she said, "I was too distracted to notice the intensity of my son's gaze at that age. Not so as a grandmother! I said to him, 'Ted, what are you thinking about?'

"He told me, 'I'm thinking about being grown up.' Just imagine, I thought, a five-year-old thinking about being all grown up! So I asked, 'What's it like, being grown up?'

"'It's great!' Ted said. And what is so great about it?

"'Being a paleontologist!' Ted declared. I was astounded that Ted knew the word *paleontologist*, let alone could pronounce it."

But she wasn't, as she explained to me, surprised by the context of this conversation. This grandmother and her grandson, Ted, were on their way to the science museum because it was Ted's favorite place from the time he was six months old. When Ted was two, he would play around the limestone cliffs near their home, gazing at the shards of limestone that had the clear imprint of ancient fossils on them. Even at two, Ted was curious about everything he saw on the limestone shards and on the cliffs themselves.

"One of my delights," Ted's grandmother added, "is seeing the world through Ted's eyes and listening to what he's thinking about. I never had time to do this with my kids. Four of them were born within two years of each other and our household was like Grand Central Station at five o'clock in the afternoon—all the time!"

Grandparents tend to have much more time to listen to their grandchildren and follow their focus and interests. Grandparents cannot know what their grandchildren will turn out to be but, for now, it is enough to pay attention and see the world as their grandchildren see it: wonderful and new.

"Have I told you about my grandchildren?"

"No. And I want you to know I appreciate it."

Anonymous

Rejoice in the Freedom of Grandparenting

- Introduce your grandchildren to things that have been enjoyable for you; for example:

  Reading: Children love to be read to. You can introduce them to your favorite stories.

  Movies and Plays: If your city has a children's theater or when a great movie comes to town, you could attend these together.

- Grandchildren enjoy accompanying you as you make things. Help them learn how to do things you enjoy such as woodworking, painting, planting a garden, cooking, or knitting.

- Observe and listen to your grandchild's interests and nurture them; for example:
  - If she or he may have been born with melodic gifts you could provide music lessons or take them to concerts. (Be sure to clear this with the parents so they support the cacophonous sounds coming from a trumpet or violin when the child is first practicing.)
  - If she or he has a love of horses, you might provide riding lessons or get them a subscription to a horse magazine.
  - If they are interested in science or math you could take them to science museums or purchase subscriptions to scientific magazines for them.
  - Nature is a great teacher. You could take them camping or on nature trail hikes. Local hiking groups, ornithology clubs, and biking clubs would be happy to either have you accompany them or arrange for a special excursion.
  - If you love to travel and you love history or art, you could arrange for discount travel trips for just you and your grandchildren.

"ANSWER: NO MATTER WHAT THE CHILD DOES, ONE COMPLAINS AND THE OTHER BRAGS."

"QUESTION: WHAT IS THE DIFFERENCE BETWEEN A PARENT AND A GRANDPARENT?"

Lois Wyse

A Day at the Races With Poppy and Grannan

Tom and Annette are active grandparents of two grandchildren, Brianna and Tommy. Brianna is fourteen going on thirty-five, and Tommy is nine and thinks it's the greatest age to be. Tommy lives in the same neighborhood as Tom and Annette. Brianna lives with her mom back East.

Tommy is "just adorable" according to his grandparents. "I'd give my life for that kid," says Annette. "Brianna, well, I'd sacrifice for her too, but I wouldn't be happy about it, and she could give a rip if I did! She is a difficult kid to warm up to, a real know-it-all." Annette sighs. "Maybe when she's on her own, she'll grow out of it."

"We sure had fun trying to help her grow out of it," says Tom. "Maybe I should say, we're trying to show her a broader world, one she'll be exposed to sooner or later."

"With Tommy," says Annette, "we just have fun. I taught him how to pitch cards in a hat under the coffee table when he was just four. We both go bike riding with him and play whiffleball. Now it's baseball."

"Anyway, we found out early that he likes numbers and horses as much as I do. So I taught him how to play blackjack and poker. Now, I'm good, but at nine years old, he's better than I am. I just get a kick out of teaching him how to bet on the horses. I have to admit, I get a kick out of getting a rise out of our conservative kids too. How our daughter and son got to be as narrow as they are, I'll never understand."

"Well," Annette sighs, "they must be somewhat indulgent because they let us take the kids to the track."

"That's true," adds Tom. "I taught Tommy how to play responsibly. I give him ten dollars in his left pocket and tell him he gets to keep his winnings in his right pocket. But when the money's gone, that's it! You only get to bet money you can afford to lose. I showed him how to analyze a race. Then I taught him how to place bets: win, place, show, exacta, trifecta, and the like. He learned a truth about wagering right away: you win some and you lose some. But it was all very fun to Tommy.

"The next weekend, Brianna came from back East to visit. Brianna's parents sent her out to the Midwest to her outrageous grandparents for a Memorial Day visit. All during the weekend Brianna's face broadcast what an ordeal this visit was for her. Her glower deepened when we announced we were going to make it a day at the races."

Annette continues, "Brianna was wearing a long cotton dress to go with her disapproving expression. I could hear her sighing in the back seat. In the rearview mirror I could see her staring out the car window, headphones on her ears so she could drown out the sound of our voices. Her sulky look seemed to ask, 'How did I get stuck with this weird family?'

"Tommy, on the other hand, was oblivious. He asked her to take off her headphones and listen while he told her how to bet on the horses. I looked in the back again, and I could see her shoulder jammed against the car door. She was rolling her eyes as Tommy tried to explain the exacta and trifecta to her. 'That's okay, Brianna,' Tommy said, 'If you can't figure it out, just do what Poppy does, and you'll win!'"

"It was a long day I'm sure for Brianna, who tried hard to hide her growing interest in the races and the fact that her ten-dollar bet was growing before her eyes and bulging out of her right pocket. At the end of the day, Brianna and Tommy were issued checks for $58.90 for an exacta pick. I yelled, 'Oh, this is great, let's get a picture. Here we go,' I said as I pointed the camera at them. 'Hold up those winning checks,' I urged.

"The next day we picked the photo up from the overnight developer. In the picture, Tommy's smile is as wide as the horizon and his $58.90 check is clearly displayed across his chest. Brianna's expression is sour. She is holding her check as low as she can, hoping it won't get in camera range and will never be read by a living soul."

Tom sighs himself and concludes, "We are having so much fun with these kids. It's great being free enough to just enjoy them. It's so important to remember what it's like to be nine years old or even fourteen and let them know you understand and love them no matter what."

Every generation revolts against its fathers and makes friends with its grandfathers.

Lewis Mumford

Michael's First Bird

When my teenage grandson expressed interest in going hunting with me, his grandfather, I was almost more excited about it than he was. After passing his gun safety course at age thirteen, Michael was eager to get out in the field.

In mid-December that year, we planned to drive to Iowa for pheasant hunting. Unfortunately, the day we picked was unusually cold, windy, and snowy.

With two longtime hunting companions, Michael and I decided to brave the elements and head out anyway. Duke, the Labrador retriever, was along for flushing and retrieving duties. As we traveled from Minneapolis, Michael repeatedly spoke of his hopes for getting a shot at a pheasant.

When we arrived in the field and got out of the truck to start hunting, I took one look at Michael and realized he was not dressed warmly enough for severe weather. So, all three adults took off something of their own to give him some protective layers.

Michael made no complaint about the biting cold, the difficulty walking through deep snow, or the few pheasants seen. He seemed quite happy just to be there.

As the day went on, everyone except the dog was increasingly uncomfortable in the wind and cold. Michael finally admitted that he'd like to sit in the truck for a minute to get warm.

Just before he could head back, however, Duke flushed a cock pheasant at my feet, too close for me to get off a shot. The bird flew toward Michael. His twenty-gauge boomed, but the pheasant was still flying. A second shot brought the rooster down for Duke to retrieve. Our elation over Michael's first bird warmed everyone up, but Michael most of all. Both grandfather and grandson were proud.

The mist in my eyes at that moment was not from the wind.

When I was a full-time physician I didn't have the freedom to have as many of these special moments with my own kids. But now, it's a joy to have this freedom to share special moments with Michael and my other grandchildren.

Joseph Tambornino

GRANDPARENTING IS A WONDERFUL TIME OF LIFE. FINALLY WE CAN HAVE THE ICE CREAM WITHOUT FIRST EATING THE VEGETABLES.

Lois Wyse

3

Offer Your Grandchildren a Legacy of Wisdom

FOR THE IGNORANT, OLD AGE IS WINTER;

FOR THE LEARNED, IT IS THE HARVEST.

Hasidic saying

One thing we learned in our interviews with many grandparents and grandchildren about their relationships was that, other than love, the gift of wisdom of the grandparents was most cherished. Wisdom is a legacy greater than property, stocks, or money because it is something that nourishes our lives and gives meaning, direction, and understanding. Property will tarnish, stock will crash, and money flows away like water. But the understanding, perception, and depth of meaning our wise grandparents give us endure long after we go to the other side of paradise.

We listened to the voices of many cultures who have lived and flourished in America, from Native Americans to Chinese, to Hispanic, to African, to European. The voices we heard told the same truths, but as Emily Dickinson would say, told them at a "slant." There were slight distinctions in the refracted rays of our lights of truth. More often than not, though, there was a wonderful unity of voices. And we learned that the acquisition and passing on of wisdom's ways is dynamic.

We are becoming, as the Reverend Cecil Murray of Los Angeles says, "one world—one people." We are all the children of God. The gift we bring as grandparents is wisdom, most often heard in our stories. If our stories are truly wise, they transcend time, culture, and religion, and so unite our grandchildren and us with humanity.

At a conference on wisdom, a Maori shaman said, "In our tribe, when a young person comes into puberty, we send them away to the grandparents, aunties, and uncles who will instruct them in how they can grow to a healthy maturity. It is not possible for them to become the individuals they are to become while they are still in the care of their parents because they are still too tied to their parents. If they try to break away (to become their own mature individuals) the tension between them and their parents will be too strong. They will never mature."

In response, one harried mother of teenagers said, "That's what I need to do, engage my wise older sister and my parents in raising these kids up!"

Similarly, a Native American Anishinabe woman married to a Lakota man observed that among the Lakota, the grandparents customarily take their grandchild who is entering his or her teenage years under instruction. She explained: "The simple reason is the parents are still too preoccupied with their own issues, coping with parenthood and trying to do meaningful work in the world, and making their marriage strong. So the grandparents, who have the perspective of experience, love of the grandchild, and a heritage of wisdom from our ancestors, are the ones who can be the most effective mentors to our young people. They are the ones who are the keepers of tradition and values."

There are many stories of African American grand-mothers who have been teachers and counselors to their grandchildren, filling in as parents if their children are sick or finishing school, or have passed away.

Because of better health care, financial stability, and education, grandparents are living longer. So it is more and more common that a child may have the opportunity to receive the wisdom of a wider circle of authority than ever before: parents, grandparents, and great-grandparents. The grandparents we spoke with listed some of the best gifts of wisdom that they believe should be passed on:

> *Spiritual lessons.* Grandparents, because of experience, can be excellent spiritual guides and counselors. Grandparents are models of the fine art and practice of contemplation and listening. By sharing their past experiences or just by their behavior, grandparents model for their grandchildren ways to face fear, resolve difficulties, and love others. Included in the top five list among all cultures were generosity, kindness, respect for all living things, gratitude, and calmness.

> *Change.* Our grandfather, Edward Rogers, gave us a perspective about how fast technological advancement could happen when he said, "When I was a teenager [he was born in 1876], it took me three days to ride my horse from my home on Sandy Lake to Minneapolis, a distance of 220 miles. Today [1961] I drive an air-conditioned Chrysler the same distance in three hours!" Today's grandparents have a special gift of having witnessed the first computers, space flights, fast foods, e-mail, and cell phones. They can guide their grandchildren through the rapids and shoals of change.

Courage. The gift of courage can lead us to a new way of thinking and being. "One of the things I noticed about both my grandmother and my mother as they grew older was that their inward vision expanded. For example, my mother was a scientist. She was always keeping up with new findings about the universe and about fellow human beings. She was also the first in our family to take the lead in understanding and embracing social changes. She accepted gay people and interracial marriage as gracefully as she did new findings in astrophysics and cracking open the mysteries of the universe!"

Happy memories. Time with grandparents can become happy memories for grandchildren. One young woman remarked, "Going to Gran's house was always exciting. You could smell the aroma of wonderful food being prepared for us as you got off the elevator to run to her condominium door. She'd always be waiting for us with a warm hug and kiss. Then we'd come into her inviting living room, furniture all polished and gleaming and books neatly stacked in her den. We'd sit down and talk about what she'd been reading or what was in the news. She'd encourage us to think for ourselves and she'd share her observations and her wisdom. She always made us feel important and grown-up." In other words, warm moments and kind words will embed the values and wisdom grandparents have to share and can provide needed strength in difficult times.

Calmness and peace. Grandchildren report that they feel secure and content in a grandparent's presence because their grandparents approach life with a sense of calm confidence. For grandchildren wounded by stress or trauma, being with a grandparent can be a healing experience.

Sharing the legacy of wisdom with your grandchildren brings joy to you and a rich storehouse of strength to them.

I'M IN MY ANECDOTAGE.

Clare Boothe Luce

Offer Your Grandchildren a Legacy of Wisdom

- Make a keepsake book for each of your grandchildren. In the book describe what your parents and grandparents were like and record their wise sayings and describe the values they cherished. Add comments about the special characteristic strength you see in your grandchild. Give the book to each grandchild to browse through once a year on his or her birthday. It could be given at other special occasions as well.

- Create a videotape of your parents, aunts, and uncles in which each person speaks about the abiding family values they would like their children to know.

- Plant a tree with your grandchild. Show reverence for that tree by caring for it well. Name the plant or tree after your grandchild.

- Bring from storage things that can be shown to teach your grandchild about history and lessons learned.

- List favorite sayings of your ancestors, like:
    - "It's better than a poke in the eye with a sharp stick, isn't it? It could be worse!"
    - "Don't tell anyone anything you wouldn't want shouted from the highest steeple at noon!"
    - "You've got another thing coming!"
    - "Go ask your father, but wait until I tell him what to say!"
    - "Don't judge another until you've walked a mile in their moccasins."
    - "Surround yourself with friends who know how to love, uplift you and will stand by you in a storm."
    - "Begin every day fresh and find joy and meaning everywhere."
    - "Never let the sun go down on your anger."

I AM LUMINOUS WITH AGE.

Meridel Le Sueur

In Two Worlds

M y grandfather straddled two worlds and five generations. He was born in 1876 in a sugar maple camp where his ancestors, the Anishinabe or "First People," had lived for several generations after they migrated from Madeline Island on Lake Superior. It was from his mother and grandmother that he learned values that sustained him throughout his nearly 100 years of life.

Papa Rogers, as we grandchildren called him, married a beautiful young woman, our grandmother, whom we called Bada. Bada was the daughter of European aristocracy and a Roman Catholic. Their marriage made headlines. Shortly after they were married, they bought a home in Minneapolis where all my grandmother's friends and extended family were located. There my grandfather began legal practice with a corporate law firm.

In the fall of the first year of their marriage, my grandfather's father died suddenly and, as his representative, my grandfather was called back to the North Country to settle his affairs. My grandfather and grandmother moved into temporary housing in a frontier environment in the village of Walker, Minnesota, on Leech Lake. They lived there for the next sixty-seven years.

Their first Thanksgiving in Walker set the tone of generosity and hospitality that would be their hallmark value for all of their days.

My grandmother was a fabulous chef. As Thanksgiving Day dawned she planned a feast and a beautifully set dining table to receive it. My grandfather went out to gather more wood for the stove at midday. When he returned he found my grandmother weeping. He was astonished and tried to console her. What could have happened?

When she was able to talk she blurted out, "All this wonderful food and this beautiful dining room, and we have no one to share it with!" She burst into tears again.

As my grandfather continued to try to comfort her, there came a knock at their kitchen door. My grandfather got up, wondering who it could be. They weren't expecting anyone.

Papa opened the door and on the front step stood a very thin man, a day's worth of stubble on his face, holding his hat in his hands and shivering. "Please sir," he said, "could you please share some bread with me. I'm traveling and have no food."

Papa clapped him on the back and said, "We can do better than that. Come in, please!"

The man was amazed. "I don't want to disturb you." But his protests were squelched by my grandfather's arm around his shoulders as he was propelled into my grandmother's aromatic kitchen.

My grandfather called out to my grandmother, "We have a guest to share our bounty with!"

My grandmother ran into the kitchen, saw the awestruck man, his hat still in his hands, threw her arms around him and said, "You are a miracle! Please come share our Thanksgiving with us."

From then on, especially through the horrible Depression years, our grandparents' house was marked by men traveling cross country in boxcars on their way to a job or a better opportunity. That meant they could always count on my grandmother to provide food for the journey. It was a merger of two worlds. Her devout mother had taught my grandmother that a stranger, especially if she or he was poor, was often an angel in disguise. Furthermore, everyone entering my grandparents' homes was to be treated as Christ.

My grandfather's ancestors had a similar belief and legend. The Anishinabe people tell the story of a boastful hunter who killed as many animals as he could to show off his skill as a hunter. Not only was he contemptible for his boasting, but he killed animals for sport. One day his boasting and selfishness became too extreme, and he was given a lesson still told to young children today. He went on a hunt for three days and found nothing to kill, not even a mouse. Whereupon an elder appeared to him, took him on a fast-paced journey to her home, sat him down, and looked through him to his discomfort.

He asked her why she stared so. "Because I wonder what kind of man you are to kill every being in sight and never share your food with those who go hungry."

He didn't like to hear that, but respectfully kept silence. The Elder then fed him *mahnomen* (wild rice) and dried fish until he was satisfied. He fell into a deep sleep, and when he awakened, he was back in his village. As he was wondering how this could have happened, a large buck appeared.

This time, the hunter begged the deer's forgiveness, killed him with one shot and brought him back where he made a great feast for his family and all his neighbors. No one went hungry. Never again did the hunter go hungry. The moral: If you share your food and are generous with others, especially those who are hungry, you will never want for anything.

To this day, our families—in the sixth generation—always host someone who is away from their home on holidays. Every guest is treated as though she or he were the Messiah.

HE WHO HAS FED A STRANGER MAY

HAVE FED AN ANGEL.

The Talmud

I Want That in My Life

Indeed, as far as our grandchildren go, actions do speak louder than words. There are other times when a question or a chance comment we make guides a grandchild's values for the rest of her life.

Because Papa died when I was still very young, I don't remember many details about him, but there is one time I will never forget. Papa decided he needed to shore up his liquor cabinet for a party he and Gran were hosting. So he took me along with him to Haskells, his favorite liquor store in downtown

Minneapolis. After the clerk rang up Papa's purchase, he reached over to a glass candy jar next to the cash register, pulled the glass top off the candy jar, drew out a red Tootsie Pop lollipop, and gave it to me.

How could that man have known the Tootsie Pop was my favorite? I wondered.

On the way back home in Papa's car, I relaxed back in the soft leather passenger seat and savored the moment. I was just thinking about how good the chocolate nougat center would taste after I ate the red candy coating on the outside when Papa turned and asked me, "Are you going to give that to your little brother?"

"No," I thought, "this is mine!" Instead I asked him, "Why?"

"Because," Papa said, "the best gift you can give to someone else is the one we want for ourselves."

I've always remembered that because it was one of my first lessons Gran and Papa taught me about generosity. Of all the people I've met growing up and in my travels, I've never met anyone as generous or thoughtful as Papa and Gran always were. That kind of magnanimous generosity is not something you see much of today. I want that in my life. I would like to be like them.

You may wonder if I gave my Tootsie Pop to my little brother. Well, I didn't. I still have it. I kept it to remind myself of Papa and his lesson.

Cynthia Hipwell

IF NOTHING IS GOING WELL, CALL YOUR GRANDMOTHER.

Italian proverb

4

Help Your Grandkids by Helping Their Parents

WE NEED TO PRACTICE THE ART OF GUIDANCE WITHOUT CLAIMS, THE CAPACITY TO MAKE SUPPORTIVE SUGGESTIONS RATHER THAN INTERFERING.

Eda LeShan

If we want to help our grandchildren, the best way is often by respecting, encouraging, and helping their parents, our children. This applies to many practical areas of raising children: for example, filling in with transportation for the grandkids, babysitting so that the parents can have a night out, helping with special events, or just listening to your child and his or her spouse when they need a friendly ear. While grandparents must be clear about boundaries on their time and money (see Chapter 6) the help they provide their own children is of great benefit to their grandchildren.

In order to help the parents, grandparent-diplomacy—the ability to help quietly but effectively—is required. This is an art that needs to be learned in order to preserve our relationship with our children and thus our grandchildren.

Grandparent diplomacy is particularly important when it comes to disciplining children. That's the parents' job, not ours. Besides, we may have lots to learn because child-rearing practices and knowledge about human development are evolutionary. Today, we are constantly learning new insights into child rearing. These insights come from psychological and sociological research and our collected human wisdom. For example, stage and screen actress Helen Hayes wrote about one development: "We, as grandparents, have to be reschooled. . . . [T]he new father figure should find a counterpart in the grandfather. . . nurturing the child is now as much a part of the father's role as it is the mother's. The authoritarian is becoming a relic."

Conscientious young parents keep abreast of new child-rearing information and studiously apply it. In support of the parents, conscientious grandparents need to join them in examining new insights. However, grandparents can diplomatically add one more dimension. They reflect about their own parent-child relationships and consider what they might have done differently. Again, Helen Hayes declared, "We can try to understand what happened to us as children, and what kind of parents we were, and we can become new, improved grandparents."

Our friend Mike Fargione, a new grandfather, observes, "One of the great things about being a grandfather is that your children now understand what you, as a parent, went through, and you can become closer than ever before. They adapt my old rules about keeping the kids safe, setting boundaries, then let the kids explore. One more thing: It's important to be respectful about what our daughter-in-law and son believe about child rearing. What they say goes, even if I don't think it's important."

We want our children to know we support and love them. And, God knows, parenting is not getting easier. It's a common cry that's also true. Add to the mix the other pressures on parents today like the fluctuating economy, global threats, and both parents working, and these parents can become quickly frazzled and sometimes desperate. It's hard to have the presence, patience, care, and wisdom to parent well when we are at loose ends.

For example, a friend of ours, after failing the bar exam for her law license, became depressed and took it out on her rambunctious kids. Her father called her and invited her to a ball game like he did when she was young. It was a dull game, which gave her dad an opportunity to tell her, "You know how proud your mother and I are of you, and we love you. Does it really matter so much if you never pass that exam?" She said it did. It was all she ever wanted to do. So her dad offered to take the kids for the summer, so she could work with tutors and be free of worrying about her children. Passing the exam helped her and ultimately the grandkids also.

WHAT'S THE BEST THING A GRAND-
MOTHER CAN DO FOR HER GRAND-
CHILD? THE ANSWER IS, "RESPECT
HER MOTHER."

Mike Fargione

Help Your Grandkids by Helping Their Parents

- Practice the art of attentive listening. Learn to have a gentle relaxed silence with your son or son-in-law/daughter or daughter-in-law. Attentive, relaxed silence is especially helpful to young parents even when they're asking for your advice when they are having difficulties. Mirror back to them the words they say in a non-judgmental tone so they can complete the thought and work it through. Always be sensitive and learn when to speak and not to speak. Refrain from giving advice.

- Learn the Native American way of telling stories about someone in a similar predicament and what they did or didn't do to solve the problem.

- If the problem or dilemma is around something you feel you may have mishandled when you were a parent, tell your children. If appropriate, ask their forgiveness. Tell them what you would now do.

- Support your children in seeking professional medical or counseling help if needed.

- Review your own childhood in an effort to understand how you were molded and how that affected your principles and beliefs. Were there things you'd change? Are there positives you brought to your parenting that you'd like to see endure? Conversely, are there beliefs you now see were negative?

- Think about your grandparents' relationship and behavior around your parents. What were the positive things your grandparents did to help your parents raise you and your siblings?

- Rather than guessing about how you can help your children and their spouses, ask them. Offer help if and only if you are willing and able to cheerfully give assistance. If they ask and you cannot help, be sure to explain carefully the reasons why you cannot assist.

- Practice diplomacy with supportive words. Find ways to praise the parents. This is lighting the candle rather than cursing the darkness.

YOUNG PEOPLE ARE THE PIONEERS
OF NEW WAYS. SINCE THEY FACE
TOO MANY TEMPTATIONS IT WILL
NOT BE EASY TO KNOW WHAT'S
BEST. . . . PERHAPS THERE WILL BE A
DAY YOU WILL WANT TO SIT BY MY
SIDE ASKING FOR COUNSEL.

Chief Dan George

The Gift Horse

"Grandpa," Rory asked, "when did you win your first blue ribbon at the state Fair?"

"Now, how did you know about that?" I asked.

"Mom showed me," she replied. "We were cleaning the attic and she came across an old scrapbook in one of the trunks. Mom showed me pictures of you on a Morgan pony. You were wearing Jodhpur pants and boots, a hacking coat, and a soft hat. The horse was at parade rest, and it wore a blue ribbon on the side of its bridle."

I couldn't help but smile, whether at the memory or at Rory's transparent interest, I couldn't be sure. "Ten," I said. "I would have been ten that first State Fair, just about the age you are now."

Rory grinned. "Just what I thought," she said.

"Grandpa?"

"Ahmm?" I murmured as if I didn't know what was coming next.

"Don't you think I'm old enough to have a horse?"

"There's a lot of responsibility with a horse," I said, trying to evade her canvassing effort, which would inevitably line me up as her ally against our common opponent, her father and my son.

"But you did it Grandpa," she protested. Then in a rush Rory ticked off her arguments. "I'm as tall as I'll ever be and my muscles are like a young colt; the doctor says so. I've got a job delivering papers so I can pay for feed. Mr. Bergemann says I can help stock shelves at the grocery so I can pay for the vet bills. I can board the horse at my friend Annie's. She says there's an extra stall in the barn where she keeps her Palomino, Golden Boy. And she says there's a saddle and tack in the barn that Scott Fine just left behind when he went to college last fall."

It was hard to say no to Rory. Her intense interest in horses was exactly like my own at her age. On the other hand, her father—in fact none of my children—had any desire to care for horses or livestock when they were growing up. Sure, they were good kids and helped out. But they all specialized in engineering in college.

The grandkids, on the other hand—they were keen about working with me. They came out every holiday and in the summers. They begged me to hang on to the farm, just for them. Funny how these interests jump generations. At any rate, that's all in the past. There came a year when crop and livestock profits were so low I couldn't see my way to pay back the bank loan I'd taken against the year's yield. That was the same year a housing tract developer made me an offer, like they say, that I couldn't refuse. The land was worth more sold than it was to grow things. I couldn't wait for one of the grandkids to take over the farm.

I could see Rory's point though. Rory had started to lobby for a horse when she was five or six. Her dad argued her down: "She is too small, we can't afford it, it's just a passing fancy, her interest won't hold."

But I picked up something different. It was more than her reading *Black Beauty* over and over or watching cowboy movies and drawing pictures of horses that plastered her bedroom walls. It was a look she'd get listening to a gallop beat in a symphony or another piece of music.

"What do you see, when you hear that music?" I asked her.

"Movement. A horse cantering. It's like I'm riding with the wind on a hard sand beach," she said breathlessly.

So on impulse I gave her a gift subscription to the *Western Horseman* magazine for her birthday and ignored my son's scowls when she squealed with delight. Later that year I took her riding at one of the livery stables outside of town and I have to tell you my chest filled with pride when I saw how quick she was to learn fundamentals. The kid was a natural.

So that afternoon, I screwed up the courage to talk to my son on Rory's behalf. It was tough. I love my son but it's like we're from different planets. Worse, he feels like I'm interfering with his role as a parent if I even make a suggestion. So I didn't want to kill Rory's chances for a horse of her own. I was careful. I talked about how Rory was maturing fast, how her world was going to expand sooner than a blink of an eye. And how she was already a head turner down at school soccer games. That got his attention.

Then I threw in the punch: "She's still interested in horses, not boys. Yet. If she could get really involved, not just renting some old nags every once in a while, we'd never have to worry about where she was or who she was keeping company with." I thought about pushing the angle of taking the horse to college or getting prepped for competition, but I stopped while I was ahead and let him mull it over.

When I came down for breakfast the next day, I overheard my son ask Rory, "If you could have anything in the world for your birthday, what would it be?" There was a long pause. "You can tell me, Rory," my son said.

"Well, you can't afford it, but I could help. I'd take another job to help pay for it." I held my breath.

"Yes?" my son asked.

"I'd really like a horse like Grandpa had when he was my age."

"Morgans are kind of hard to find, Rory, but we can try." I heard him say.

"Well, if that doesn't beat all," I thought. Could it be that Rory's mom was in on this too or maybe my son wasn't the stubborn old mule I thought he was?

My son told Rory, "School's still number one. So taking another job and taking care of a horse at the same time would make it tough to keep up with your schoolwork. Tell you what, let's see what all this is going to come to; not just money, but your time too. And, we'll make up a budget and a calendar together. Mom and I have talked it over. We'll start a loan for you, which you can pay back over time. We'll review how it's going for you every month. If this takes you away from school or your friends, or the job's not working, we need to give up the horse."

I heard her scream with joy and her feet hit the floor as she bounded into her mom and dad's embrace. "I will work it out, just watch me," she shouted.

I really couldn't see for the tears. I blew my nose loudly so they'd know I was in the hall. I walked in the kitchen to see my son's face as he caressed his daughter. He gave me a huge smile like the sun just rose in the sky. "Thanks, Dad," was all he had to say.

Rory was as good as her word. She followed my footsteps and won every event she entered at the state fair and university horse meets. Then, prior to her junior year in college, she faced the hardest choice anyone who loves horses has had to make. She had been trail riding with friends. Her Morgan was cantering easily over unfamiliar prairie terrain and stepped hard on a mound made by some borrowing animal. Rory heard a snap. The horse stumbled and pitched her hard over his neck. Rory was fine, but her beloved Morgan was not. Like many of his breed, he was gallant and walked the distance back to the barn, Rory leading him. The vet's examination was thorough, his verdict grim. The fracture was such that the Morgan in his opinion should never be ridden again. At his age, the vet said, he should be put down.

Rory couldn't accept this. She tried all kinds of treatments. Another vet thought that the Morgan could take light riding but not, as he had in the past, an adult rider or anything other than light walking. He gently suggested Rory consider visiting Vineland, a center for children with handicaps, to see if the Morgan could adapt to work with children. She went and became keenly drawn to the connection between the children and horses. The Morgan took to the kids like a charm. He adapted to their tempo and needs.

For her part, Rory volunteered at Vineland all summer and three times a week when college was in session. That way she could stay close to her Morgan and focus her new interest in the kids.

My granddaughter Rory is now in her third year of medical school. She aims to be a child psychiatrist. Morgan is the oldest horse of his breed on record. I aim to match him. I want to be there when Rory hangs out her shingle and someday lets me take her own daughter or son, my great-grandchild, riding for the first time!

BEING A GRANDFATHER IS STEPPING

OUT INTO THE DAWN.

Victor Hugo

The Link

For me, becoming a grandfather was just magic. What stands out is the link between my father and me and now between my son and me. While we've never talked about it, the bond and affection between my son and me has grown even stronger.

For background, I should tell you a little bit about our relationship, father and son, before Matt was married.

I was a protective father around my children, and Matt tested the very limits. He was the most daring kid I've ever known. He knew no fear, ever. For example, the first time I took the kids to a ski lodge, Matt took one lesson, skied the beginner hill, mastered it, then couldn't wait to ski Black Diamonds, also called Kamikaze Run.

I'd have to literally rein him in. He was also our first kid who was bold enough to drop out of college for a year. He wanted to see the world, coach skiing, and hang out. I had trouble with that. I was happy to support him while he paid attention to his education, but I was darned if I'd support his frolic. That was okay with him. He worked at a ski lodge out East then struck out on a cross-country exploration. When he reached the West Coast, he'd done everything he wanted to do and returned to college with new zeal the next fall.

He didn't wait to get married either. As soon as he and Susan graduated, they married, started their teaching jobs, and got pregnant. Baby Chris was born in the spring on the East Coast. My wife Janet and I couldn't sleep because we were so excited to see him. But I had to wrap up some contract work, and Janet's school was winding up its term. So we had to wait three weeks before we could see him. I admit I had some concerns about how Matt would be as a parent. I had every confidence in Susan. But I was worried about whether

Matt's boisterous, fearless ways might just cascade into his parenting. I was soon to find out the answer.

We arrived for our first visit to see the baby on a spectacular spring day. Baby Chris was a bright-eyed, strong, alert little boy, and we fell madly in love with him from the very start. We played with him, got to settle him into his crib, then we hit the sack ourselves for much needed sleep.

When we awoke, Matt had already been up feeding Chris and had our breakfast ready for us. "I have an idea, Pop," he said. "Let's pack a picnic lunch and take him to Overlook Park. It's great weather and a picnic will be like old times!" I agreed in a heartbeat.

On the way over to Overlook, Janet and I wanted to take turns holding the baby, but Matt and Susan insisted he be placed backwards in what felt like a fifty-pound car seat. "Safety regulations," they said. Their look toward us already had a questioning gaze like, "Do these two old ducks even know what they're doing?"

We ate a leisurely lunch and watched the birds and people walk by. Matt, Susan, and Janet stretched out on our army blankets to rest and drink in the sun. Soon everybody but Baby Chris and I were napping. Now, I've always wondered, what does a baby see, what do they think when they first go out in the world? Well, I just spontaneously picked up Baby Chris, bundled him up, because it started to turn windy, and took him for a long walk. He was perfectly alert and focused on everything I pointed out to him.

I felt like I had been reborn with this wondrous child, and I was getting to see the world new again. We must have been gone about an hour before we circled back to the picnic site. Just as we came into view of the site I saw Matt racing toward us, a look of frantic worry on his face.

He was about twenty feet from us as I heard him shouting at me, "Pop, where have you been?" He rushed up to me, took Chris from my arms, fixed a steely parental eye on me and said, "Pop, don't you ever take off with the baby again without telling me exactly where you're going and for how long!" In that moment, I knew my father's and my fatherly protective torch had been passed to a new generation. I've been proud of Matt before, and always filled with love for him, but never as much as in that moment. I had helped little Chris after all.

JUST AS YOU'RE GOING TO HAVE YOUR OWN STYLE OF GRANDPAR-ENTING THAT SUITS YOU, YOUR CHIL-DREN WILL HAVE THEIR OWN STYLE OF PARENTING. YOU ARE NOT THERE TO COACH (UNLESS ASKED), BUT TO BE A CHEERLEADER.

Ruth Westheimer and
Steven Kaplan

5

Admit It!
You're Going to Have Favorites

ONE THING TO REMEMBER (IF WE
START FEELING GUILTY) OUR
CREATOR PUT US TOGETHER THIS
WAY. WE ARE NATURALLY DRAWN
TO SOME PEOPLE. OTHERS AREN'T
SO ATTRACTIVE TO US. THEN THERE
ARE THOSE WE CAN HARDLY STAND
TO BE AROUND. THAT'S TRUE OF THE
GENERAL POPULACE, THE NEIGH-
BORS, AND KINFOLK OF EVERY KIND.
EVEN GRANDCHILDREN.

Charlie W. Shedd

"Mom, which grandchild do you like the best?"
Without skipping a beat, Lorraine, a West
Virginia widowed mother with eight children and ten
grandchildren, answered, "The one who's sick, the one
who's far away, or the one who's in trouble."

In the 1960s, the comedy team of Tom and Dick Smothers were sure to get a laugh from this line: "Mom always liked you best." People laughed because who among us hasn't felt either the privilege or the jealousy of being in a favored position? On the other hand if, as a parent, you have bent over backwards trying to be fair in your attentions, affections, gifts, and other support of your children, you might be irritated at the suggestion that one child was favored over another.

Let's face it, one of the pleasures of being a grandparent is that you don't have to restrain yourself any more. You can indulge in the real bond you have with a certain grandchild. It doesn't mean you love the others less, it just means that there exists between you and a certain grandchild a golden thread of understanding and appreciation beyond words. It's a phenomenon that is unpredictable. And more often than not, that relationship starts with the grandchild.

Before the grandchild's behavior can be prescribed, his tiny arms reach out for a grandfather or grandmother. Their eyes lock in mutual recognition, or the grandchild will squeal and laugh, kick and leap toward the grandparent. The infant chooses the object of his or her delight and, when it's reciprocated, it forges a bond that may last forever.

We know a young mother who, when doing routine errands and respectful of her mother's need for a day of quiet solitude, deliberately drives miles out of her way to avoid driving by her parents' house. She made the mistake of driving near her mother and father's neighborhood one day when her parents were on vacation, and her eighteen-month-old daughter began to sob, "No! No! Gran's house, Gran's house!" Her daughter was inconsolable even with her mother's explanation that Gran was far away in Florida. That explanation made matters even worse.

Another grandmother we know regularly babysat her granddaughter on Friday afternoons and evenings when her daughter and son-in-law needed time for themselves. The bond between grandmother and granddaughter grew so strong that even at eleven years old her granddaughter insists on keeping "the date with Grandma Stevenson." Even though she is now old enough to go out with her parents or school friends, "Grandma is the best!" she shouts. And Grandma agrees!

In short, try to love all your grandchildren and be as evenhanded as possible, but be honest: just admit that you will probably have favorites among your grandchildren. Even so, you can still be a confidant to grandkids who need one or a teacher to the grandchild whose parents don't have certain skills. Some of your grandkids will be your favorites and vice-versa. It's just part of the deal.

EACH OF YOUR GRANDCHILDREN IS DIFFERENT, AND THEIR NEEDS MAY VARY. . . . REMEMBER THAT IT IS ALWAYS YOU WHO DEFINES THE ROLES YOU PLAY, BASED ON THE CIRCUMSTANCES AND THE TYPE OF RELATIONSHIP YOU HAVE WITH EACH GRANDCHILD.

*Ruth Westheimer and
Steven Kaplan*

Admit It! You're Going to Have Favorites

- Reflect back on your own grandparents. Did they have clear favorites among the grandkids? How did you feel about it? Was it too obvious or skewed? How did your grandparents handle their favoritism?

- Do you have a favorite among your grandchildren? Do you have a special bond with one or two of them? How did it form and how does it manifest itself?

- Since having favorites is natural, we sometimes have to be more conscious of being evenhanded with those grandchildren who aren't our favorites. Strategize about how you can be evenhanded with all your grandkids in terms of time, gifts, and celebrations.

- Make a list of all of your grandchildren. Beside the name of each, write one special thing that you can do with that person. Be particularly aware of the children who are most troublesome. If you cannot think of anything special to do, ask their parents or ask the child himself or herself for ideas.

Treat each grandchild as an individual. Don't think you have to do or give equal things to each one.

Eleanor Berman

My Pop

Ever since Sean could crawl around, he wanted to be with his mom's daddy, whom he called "My Pop," and his mom's mother, whom he called "Gran-M." That seemed to suit everyone just fine because when Sean was born his mother, Susan, was finishing her doctoral work in agricultural economics and his dad, Pat, was just starting as a junior associate in a large metropolitan law firm.

Gran-M wanted to scale back on her practice as a therapist, and Pop announced he wanted to accept an emeritus pastor position to devote more time to writing and teaching. Sean's arrival might have been inconvenient for his parents since they didn't want to entrust him to full-time day care. Nevertheless, it was perfect timing for Gran-M who wanted to luxuriate in enjoying her first grandchild in a way she hadn't been able to do when Susan and her other children were growing up.

Pop agreed that it would be great to have Sean in their home all day on Mondays and during the weekday afternoons. Mornings and weekends saw Sean at home with his mom and dad.

The fact that Sean was their first grandchild and was given the Gaelic name Sean Patrick in honor of his grandfather (Susan's father), Jon Patrick, and that Susan and Pat insisted that Gran-M and Pop-Jon be Sean Patrick's godparents sealed their heart.

As for Sean, the attraction for his grandparents was also absolute right from the start. He became lovingly bonded with both of them. The signs were all over the place. For instance, as his parents' car approached Gran-M and Pop's cobblestone street, Sean would start jumping up and down and squeal with excitement. How Sean could know he was nearing his grandparent's house was a mystery to his parents since he was strapped into his car seat, facing backwards with his head below the window level. "Must be the bounce of the car on the cobblestones," mused Pat.

At any rate, there were other attractions at Gran-M's house too. Sean's face grew dreamy as his parents approached the back stoop and the door that opened into Gran-M's kitchen where the aroma of chocolate chip cookies or vanilla and cinnamon wafted out and surrounded him. (When he grew older Sean wondered if Gran-M used vanilla as a perfume because she always smelled delicious.) Once inside her kitchen Sean would be greeted with a big hug and kiss from Gran-M and purring from Pop's calico cat whom he called "Pole-Cat" and with whom Sean would play for hours.

Gran-M had a special room where Sean could play and take naps. The room was painted blue with soft clouds on the walls and constellations on the ceiling. There was a chest in the room filled with toys just for Sean. There were also toys loved by children who had grown up long ago, like a woolly white lamb with black ears mounted on an iron platform that had four iron wheels. One eye was missing and the lamb's tail was worn down to a nub, but that was the toy Sean loved the most.

Gran-M said it had belonged to Pop's daddy a long time ago. Every once in a while as Sean and Pop worked the carpenter shop, Sean would get lost in there as Pop's calm, meticulous ways of working with wood furniture simultaneously intrigued and lulled him.

As Sean grew older, Pop showed him how to whistle through his teeth, how to play the harmonica, and how to whittle slingshots out of box elder branches. Pop gave Sean odd jobs around the house like sweeping up wood shavings in the carpenter shop, drying dishes, carrying out garbage, and finding groceries on Gran-M's list when they went to the supermarket. Sean had a knack for gardening and soon learned how to pull weeds, hoe, and plant vegetables for succulent eating later in the summer. Pop and Gran-M paid him for his work and showed him how to keep an account book at the local bank. Sean learned lessons about saving for the future and setting some money aside for giving.

Summers meant camping out with Pop. They packed a tent, food, and cooking gear in a canoe and headed up the river. On the river Sean and Pop could yell their lungs out, sing off key, and nobody would mind. They'd swim in the river and catch their supper. Sean learned how to watch for deadheads in the river by observing the flow of water around a submerged object. They'd watch for wild animals like muskrats and beavers in the river and deer and fox on land. Pop taught Sean about the constellations in the summer sky.

As he grew into adolescence, his teachers and friends commented on Sean's humor and confidence and ease with others. His teachers particularly were amazed at the creative ways he could solve problems. "That boy's going to go far," they'd say. Sean overheard them and thought, "I never want to be so far that I can't be near Pop and Gran-M."

Every day, Sean would cut a path past Gran-M and Pop's house to check on them. As their health declined, Sean was able to pick up the slack. Initially, Pop needed to instruct Sean carefully, with quiet patience, about how to do things like change the oil or the carburetor in the car, replace the screen windows in the house for the storms, and service the furnace for winter. He was pleased to observe how Sean needed his instruction less and less and how the now strapping young man was able to take over the jobs Pop was unable to do with ease.

If teachers were amazed at Sean's problem solving, friends were amazed that jealousy wasn't a problem for Sean's parents. Some well-meaning colleagues warned Susan that in their opinion, Sean wouldn't be able to make a clean break when he went to college.

"That relationship with his grandparents might stifle him, you know," they clucked. "And what will happen if they pass on? What then?"

Susan agreed that parting was going to be hard on all of them. "I think," she said, "theirs is the most natural, loving relationship we could ever hope to know. What we've got here is the real circle of life."

Pat supported her. "I wish I had the kind of closeness Sean has with my own parents. Anybody would walk a hundred miles in the Sonoran desert barefoot for that kind of relationship. Anyway, I couldn't have given Sean the kind of lessons his grandfather has given him over the years. Just look at Sean's self-assurance and competence. We've got to count our blessings!"

Pat didn't even mind when others said that Sean seemed to prefer his grandfather over him. "He knows who his dad is," Pat said. "I'll be around a good long time; fact is I love Pop too—just the same way Sean does."

USUALLY WHEN YOU'RE REALLY CLOSE TO SOMEONE, YOUR AND THEIR HABITS CAN SET YOU OFF, AND YOU WONDER, DO I REALLY KNOW YOU? WITH GRAN, IT WAS AS IF WE COULD GET THE BEST OF EACH OTHER WITHOUT THE NEGATIVES, WITHOUT JUDGMENT AND CRITICISM.

M. Cynthia Hipwell

The Enchanted One

My name is Du Xiaoging. I was born in 1962 in China. I am the youngest of four girls in my family. Traditionally, the youngest child is called, "The Enchanted One." In my case it was doubly true. My grandmother never hesitated to admit to her closest friends that I was her favorite! "I always do more for Xiaoging," she would say.

I am told that in America all children are considered to be equal. There are no favorites. In order to be fair to everyone, American parents treat each of their children the same. But not in China. Close friends will ask the parents or grandparents, "Who is your favorite?" Usually parents will say, "The youngest, the baby." Grandparents almost always say the youngest. After all, the youngest child is "The Enchanted One."

It does cause jealousy. My grandmother and my parents gave me more attention and care. My older sisters would complain, "She always gets her way" or "It wasn't like that when we were her age."

I responded to the effect, "It isn't because they love you less." But my sisters weren't consoled. Even now, I am not easily satisfied. It is not an easy life to never be content with what one has. So what I am going to tell you may seem odd or different.

It all started when I was one year old. My father's mother, Mengtang Li, came to live in our home. It is very common in China for grandparents to be the main caretakers of their grandchildren. She lived with us until she died in 1986, when I was twenty-four. In China, we make a distinction between our father's mother, "the interior mother" who is called Popo and the "exterior mother" who is called Wai Po. We always called our grandma, "Popo."

Popo was a very small woman. She suffered a lot. At the age of twelve, she lost both her parents. She had no family, so she was sent away to another family. Imagine at twelve years old, with no family left being told by a family of strangers, as she was, "We bought you. You will work for us and marry our son." It was not a good marriage. They had two children, my father and his brother. It was much later, after my grandfather died that Popo came to live with us.

I slept with my grandmother in her bed from the time she arrived. My earliest memory of her was that she would wake up early so she could make breakfast for the whole family. I lay awake in bed hearing her start the charcoal fire for cooking and smelling the warm breakfast cooking.

At that time in China everyone was very poor. We were better off than most, but even we did not have meat more than once or twice a week. When we had meat, Popo would set some aside and hide it. After dinner, she would say, "Darling, come, I want you to help me with something." That was her way of drawing me away from the others and slipping me a piece of meat or part of her meal. She thought she was being discrete, but my sisters weren't fooled and resented it.

Later, when I went to school, I learned to read and write quickly. After school I'd come home and report right away to Popo, to see if I could help her with the household chores and also teach her what I learned. For example, I helped her with the laundry, hanging clothes on a bamboo rod. Then I would show her my writing, and soon Popo and her friends had me writing their letters for them. In her generation, women were not educated. They could neither read nor write. So my writing was a great help to them. Popo was proud of my abilities.

When I was eleven, I was sent away to a boarding school. I was lonesome for my grandmother and wrote her and my parents every day. None of my other sisters would do this. I later found out that Popo had saved every one of my letters and had them bound. When I came home for visits, she insisted on doing my laundry. When I returned to school, I had fresh clean clothes and a case full of special foods Popo made for me to supplement our poor diet at school.

I did well in school. Eventually, I was sent to university and to army service in Funjian Province, near Taiwan. When I received my first army pay I sent it to Popo. I asked her to use it to buy hearing aids because she was always a bit hard of hearing. Popo gave me so much. I could never express my gratitude enough. Perhaps, with the hearing aids, I thought, she could communicate without others having to shout at her. Maybe she would even hear songs and the sound of the wind.

I am a mother now and my own mother is a grandmother. Popo has been dead for sixteen years. There is never a day that I don't think of her. There are things about Popo I want in my own life. Most of all, I want the friends that she had. They were wonderful friends who were as honest and hospitable to others as she was. For example, if someone, even a stranger, came to our house at mealtime, she always invited them to stay, no matter what we were serving. If one of her friends was sent off to work and had no one to look after her children, Popo would care for the children as if they were her own, sometimes for a period of years! Like Popo, I will do everything I can to help my friends. And I will always think of the wants and needs of others.

Popo gave me everything she had and all her love. Her love overflowed into my life, so I can freely let it flow into the lives of my family and friends. This is how I honor her, my Popo.

Du Xiaoging

NOBODY CAN DO FOR LITTLE CHIL-
DREN WHAT GRANDPARENTS CAN
DO. GRANDPARENTS SORT OF
SPRINKLE STARDUST OVER THE LIVES
OF LITTLE CHILDREN.

Alex Haley

6

Establish Boundaries on Your Money and Time

A GRANDCHILD LOVES US FOR WHO WE ARE, NOT THE PRESENTS WE GIVE THEM. LATER IN LIFE MY GRANDCHILDREN REMEMBER THE SONGS I SANG TO THEM OR THE SPECIAL FOODS I GAVE THEM OR A DAY IN THE PARK. GIVE WHAT YOU CAN . . . YOU AND THE TIME YOU SPEND WITH THEM ARE THE MOST PRECIOUS GIFTS A GRANDCHILD CAN RECEIVE. I KNOW. I LEARNED THAT FROM MY GRANDCHILD.

Sylvia Little

Grandparenting is not the time to relive the past. It is vitally important to have a clear understanding about who is responsible for rearing the children. It is always the parents (unless the parent dies, defects, or otherwise relinquishes the role).

One frequent bone of contention that may seem like a small one, but can be just large enough to choke the breath out of many relationships, is gift giving. Why should this be a problem? Isn't indulgence part of the fun of being a grandparent?

Unbounded gift giving *can* become a problem because no grandparent can rightfully claim the primary role of provider that is the parents' alone. Take another side of the situation, grandparents who have invested their income prudently with an eye toward retirement. They were determined not to be a burden to their children and wanted to give generously to the community. One of their children thought them selfish and stingy because they didn't give elaborate presents to their grandchildren.

We all know of grandparents whose circumstances are such that they need to live quite frugally. Some parents—their children—may resent the small denomination bill slipped into a card or a homemade gift for the grandchild.

On the other hand, indulgent money and gifts from the grandparents also have the energy to polarize parents against grandparents as well as one set of grandparents against the other set.

Sometimes there are wide differences in what parents and grandparents can give at birthdays and holidays. Some parents (and the other set of grandparents) may feel humiliated by the mother lode of eye-popping gifts that grandparents give the grandchildren. And then the specter exists of parents and two sets of grandparents competing for the grandchild's affection and thinking that they can get it by showering the grandchildren with expensive presents. Once this merry-go-round begins, stopping it can be terribly difficult.

One reason this occurs is that grandparents may remember how hard it was to raise their own children. They may not have been able to afford the toys or clothes or schools they had wanted to give their children or have themselves. They may harbor a memory of wanting to achieve or have something when they were children and now project their frustrated dreams of being an actor, ballet dancer, or an equestrian on their grandchild. So they not only buy the accoutrements of these endeavors, they offer to pay for lessons. Once again, these gifts in themselves are not the problem. Conflict erupts when both grandparents and parents operate on unexamined assumptions that have not been carefully discussed.

Having said this, it is true that many young parents today may be facing greater financial stress than we did when we were raising our children. Many grandparents find that they are the anchors for their daughters or sons when a marriage dissolves, death or desertion descends, or their children lose a job. In times such as these, grandparents should certainly help as much as they can. According to experienced grandparents, the key is that the financial help doesn't create hardship that will lead us into dependency.

You may think of other scenarios in which questions of boundaries on gift giving have become an issue. In each of these cases, there has to be clear communication between the grandparents and the child's mother and father about the gifts and expectations. Clear boundaries, mutually agreed upon, can keep unintended hurt at a minimum and outright rifts completely out of the picture.

HEIRLOOMS WE DON'T HAVE IN OUR FAMILY. BUT STORIES WE'VE GOT.

Rose Chernin

Establish Boundaries on Your Money and Time

- Be clear about your feelings and motives. Be straight with the parents. If you have not had a conversation about money and time boundaries, have it. Be sure to listen as well as to speak directly.

- Find other ways to express love and care besides giving money and possessions. Make grandchildren things or give them heritage gifts, like an heirloom that is age-appropriate. Make them a gift of stories about their ancestors.

- Regularly give the gifts of praise and encouragement, which bring confidence to your grandchildren. Send cards or notes or e-mail greetings when they've done something noteworthy or just when you feel like saying hello.

- Some of us have grown so affluent that our grandchildren have no idea about how poor people have to live. Financial educator Ruth Hayden, says: "If we all would set aside ten percent for charity and five percent for savings, we would wipe out the world's poverty." Maybe you could match a child's allowance with an amount in a special savings account in which they would set aside five percent as savings and ten percent for charity. With your grandchildren, research some local or worldwide service organizations. Help them decide which charities the donation should go to each year. Then take time with each of your grandchildren and help them decide where they would like to use their individual savings. Be sure to support each one's dreams and ideas. Don't forget to include your grandchildren's parents in the planning.

- Have a frank talk with your children about your own budget strategies and your philosophy of gift giving for special occasions and holidays.

- Based on your grandchildren's special interests and after close consultation with their parents, establish a giving plan for each grandchild. For example, it might include: a savings account for tuition, clothes, books, or materials for post-high school education; a subscription to a special interest magazine; or tickets to a sporting event or concert series.

No grandparent has the right to take away from fathers and mothers the right to do their own parenting.

Charlie W. Shedd

Time: The Best Gift of All

I'd go to the ends of the earth for my grandchildren, and my children know it! Besides that, with me they get the cream of the crop of babysitters, someone who adores the children and has years of experience. And I'm cheap! They don't have to pay me.

But frankly, I started to resent all the baby-sitting I was asked to do. I resented the fact that the kids wanted to take advantage of my love and willingness to sacrifice for them. What I resented most was the assumption that I'd drop everything and take care of the children all weekend, then be exhausted going back to work on Monday. It wasn't fair to the company I work for.

The kids don't realize that even as active and healthy as I am, it's tough to heft a thirty-pound baby out of his bed and carry him about because he can't yet walk, while at the same time keep my eye on his active sister who has learned to zoom around. I'm not even mentioning the hard work of changing diapers, feeding them, playing with them and getting them down for their naps. And of course, they never sleep at the same time.

I worry about grandparents who aren't as physically able as I am caring for their grandchildren. It's plain dangerous to put the grandchildren in the care of grandparents who are not up to it for even a little while. This sounds selfish. But I've raised my children and did a good job. They're great kids and I'm happy about how they've turned out. But now, I have my home the way I want it. I work part-time in medical records and I'm enjoying life again.

The straw that broke the camel's back for me came on the weekend of my son and daughter-in-law's anniversary. That Sunday morning, when I was busy changing Todd, little Joanna—who was just learning to walk—lost her balance and fell against a pedestal that held a Lalique Crystal lovebird. It was the last gift my late husband gave me for our fortieth anniversary. That did it. I just sat down and cried.

So when the kids returned, I said, "We have to have a conversation." It wasn't easy because I had to get the resentment behind me first. I started by saying I really love Todd and Joanna and I do want to help out baby-sitting, but I can only baby-sit when I am able and when I want to. It was uncomfortable at first. They seemed to want to go in the direction of being hurt and feeling put upon because they didn't think they asked me to baby-sit as much as Todd's brother and sister-in-law did. But I stood firm and said that this applies to everyone.

I really wanted to avoid resentment on both sides. No one is served by my resenting being with the grandkids. Then I followed up with a plan. I agreed to baby-sit in short sessions, planned in advance, with no overnights or weekends. If they absolutely needed me in an emergency, of course I'd help out. We also worked out a contingency plan: a list of reliable babysitters who could fill in when they needed to get away for a weekend or longer stay. That way, I didn't have to worry about taxing myself or endangering the grandchildren.

This experience taught me that it's really important to have a frank conversation with the parents before the baby comes about expectations on your gift of time. It's important to be honest with ourselves first, then the kids, about how much you can do, what you're able to do, and when you'll be able to do it.

Having this conversation can help everyone concerned to avoid resentment and build mutual respect.

Karen M.

MY GRANDMOTHERS ARE FULL OF
MEMORIES
SMELLING OF SOAP AND ONIONS
AND WET CLAY
WITH VEINS ROLLING ROUGHLY
OVER QUICK HANDS
THEY HAVE MANY CLEAN WORDS TO
SAY.

Margaret Walker

Christmas Over the Top

Our parents had always gone overboard when it came to presents. So it didn't surprise me when our first child, Charles, was born that they came laden with complete layette sets, toys, and furniture. The tacitly agreed script when the bills came in was that it was due to my mother's extravagance, and my father paid the bills. Then, one year, the script and direction took a distinctly sharp turn.

It was the Christmas of 1956. My husband Joe had just finished medical school, accepted an officer's commission, and was assigned to Mountain Home Air Force Base on a windswept plain in Idaho. We were homesick for our family and dreaming of a white Christmas in Minnesota, where snowcapped trees were glistening and skaters cut figures on shimmering ice on some of the state's many lakes.

Our budget was stretched on our military salary. We had two-year-old Charles, and another baby on the way. We decided to make Christmas gifts that year. So I busied myself and buried my homesickness by making Christmas stockings for my little sisters and tablecloths and quilts for my parents and in-laws.

Our homesickness became magnified when Daddy called to tell us that Mother had been taken to the hospital with an apparent heart attack. She was getting better, but she'd have to be on bed rest for four weeks. He was "taking over" Christmas, he told us. Daddy assured us he had everything in hand and not to worry. So, we didn't until later in the week when the postman started delivering the first set of packages. He was literally dragging his boots through the snow trying to balance the heavy boxes without falling.

Out of the first set of boxes stuffed animals leaped into the room. The next were clothing boxes filled with two sets of camel hair dress coats, leggings, hats, and gloves for our son. Another was filled with four sets of snow boots, two for dress-up and two for the playground. We figured a mistake had been made in the order and resolved to send the things back. The next day the gifts were more numerous: two sets of snowsuits, two sets of trains, baby outfits to clothe quintuplets.

When we called Daddy, he assured us that there was no mistake. "I know what you kids are going through. Anyway, you know I couldn't do these things when you were small. I want to do it for you now! And remember these are *your* gifts to Charles." He emphasized *your*, an emphasis I would only understand after talking with my thirteen-year-old-sister, Priscilla.

Priscilla had overheard our parents' hushed conversation and resolution. She told me, "After last Christmas when you were here, I heard Daddy and Mom quietly talking about how terrible they felt when they saw the look on Uncle Joe's face. Remember little Charles played all day with his train set from them while completely forgetting the working steam shovel that Joe had scrimped and saved to give him. Daddy told Mom that from now on they had better be careful not to top the presents you two give to Charles. That's why Daddy went overboard this year and insisted that the presents were *your* presents to Charles. Mom kind of understands what Daddy did, but she'll take over the gift buying again for sure."

And now I understood what my father meant when he put the emphasis on *your*. Joe and I appreciated Daddy's sensitivity to our feelings, but we were also glad that Mom would be doing the buying for the next Christmas.

I'VE KNOWN A FEW GRANDMAS WHO LEFT THEIR HEAD FAR BEHIND WHEN THEY TOOK OFF FOR THE SHOPPING CENTER. BUT FROM WHAT I'VE SEEN AND EXPERIENCED FIRST HAND, THIS IS MOSTLY A GRANDFATHER AILING.

Charlie W. Shedd

7

Seize the Moment, Offer Stability in Troubled Times

SPARE ME THE TEARS THAT HAVE NO
HEALING.

Malcolm Arnold

Cherishing each moment we have in life is good advice in all circumstances. It applies well to grandparenting too. After all, as with the rest of life, we never know when troubles or even death may separate us from our beloved grandchildren.

Many versions are told of the Buddha and grieving mother who had lost her infant. The mother cried out in despair, "Why, why must I suffer so?" Buddha sent the mother on a mission to visit the homes of families all over the universe to find the answer to her question from a home not touched by suffering. When she arrived at the first home, she found a family of seven whose house, crops, barn, and animals had been consumed by fire. The family was struggling just to survive. So she stayed and helped them. Then she came to the castle of a king where his family kept vigil as he lay dying of cancer. Knowing how terrible grief could be, the grieving mother stayed to help the king and his family in their time of loss.

Her quest to find a home not visited by sorrow con-tinued unrelieved. Finally, the mother returned to the Buddha to report that nowhere did she find a home that had not been visited by sorrow and loss. However, her own grief had dissipated in her acts of compassion. And so, the grieving mother had learned the first lesson of compassion.

As we listened to the stories of grandparents, we were reminded of this important truth: No family is insulated from grief and loss. We are united in a circle of sharing the sorrows inherent in love: the loss of grandchildren to moving away, separations, divorces, and even, tragically, death. And, as grandparents reminded us in one way or another: "Make the most of the moments you have with your grandchildren. Every moment is precious."

One of the most profound losses we can experience is the death of a child or grandchild. In our own moth-er's time and until recently, the death of an infant or a young child was treated as an ordinary occurrence. A young mother was told as reassurance, "Don't worry, you will have another" or "It's for the best." Grandparents were admonished to be positive and not show their feelings about the loss of their grandchild, especially around the parents who needed to face it, pull themselves together, and get on with life.

Fortunately, as we have learned more about human development, proper respect and attention are given to grief. Grandparents, by virtue of their experience and well-earned discernment, have much to offer their chil-dren in these situations, like caring for their other grandchildren while their children receive needed counseling or rest. But most of all, grandparents can give their children and grandchildren understanding, patience, and compassion.

If grandparents have experienced the loss of a child, they will understand the howling, mad grief that engulfs their daughter and son. Reeve Lindbergh, daughter of Charles Lindbergh, writes of the strong support her mother, Anne Morrow Lindbergh, was able to give her when Reeve's son John died of a seizure related to infant encephalitis. After making the emergency call, Anne quietly insisted that she and her daughter sit with the baby next to the crib where he had fallen asleep the night before. Although Reeve Lindbergh wanted to rush from the room of her infant son, she obeyed her mother and thus began the slow terrible footsteps to grieving that would help mother and grandmother through a vale of tears and exploding grief.

Anne Morrow Lindbergh, as with mothers of her generation who lost infants, was never allowed to see the body of her own baby Charles, Jr. when it was discovered after his kidnapping and murder. Through the insights gleaned from her own grief, she was able to instruct and guide her daughter through her desperate hours.

In our own family, Grandma Herbison came immediately to my mother's side when we lost our sister Sarah shortly after her birth. Grandma Herbison did the laundry and prepared meals for me and my sisters so that my parents could grieve, and my mother could recover physically and emotionally.

Grandma helped my mother spiritually. What she did was named as a model by other grandparents whose insights we gathered: "You'll feel ready to tear the world apart. That's normal. Let it flow. Cry."

Our stiff-upper-lip grandmother encouraged it and added, "All right, if you don't want to upset the children, go somewhere where you can bawl your eyes out. Tears wash some of the pain away. Bottled up tears aggravate your stomach and give you horrible headaches. If you're angry, you have a right to be. It isn't fair. Tell God about it. Psalms are good for this. Pray if you can. You'll be able to smile again and love again. But in your own good time."

While these words are insightful and still timely, contemporary grandparents would add these suggestions for helping their children through the loss of a child:

- Seek counseling and support groups.
- Be sure to let your children know how they are loved.
- Take care of your own grandparent grief, too.

Next to the death of a child or grandchild, the next hardest loss grandparents face may be the separation or divorce of their children. Separation and divorce carry with them their own patterns of grieving. Grandparents may be caught in the throes of wondering what they did wrong while rearing their children, particularly if the apparent cause of the separation or divorce is that your married child is treating his or her family badly.

Grandparents say that it is critical that you pay attention first and foremost to the best interests of your grandchildren. That means that you need to muzzle any criticism of the offending party and bias toward one or the other parent. Other experienced grandparents caution against going to other family members to talk about the problem, as tempting as this might be. They suggest that if you, as a grandparent, are feeling swamped by conflicting feelings, a heart to heart talk with a professional counselor might be in order.

Grandparents can be the center of stability and continuity for their grandchildren. Grandparents can listen to a grandchild to help them sort out feelings, make sense of things, and cope with and adjust to new situations or developments.

Grandparents tell us they need to be on the alert for signs of distress and confusion, such as children reverting to infantile behavior or acting out if they find themselves having to move to a new home or face new schools or step-siblings. But, again, the most important point to keep in mind is the well-being of the grand-children and maintaining ties with your child who is suffering too.

One additional note on the subject of grand-parents facing separation with their grandchildren: Grandparents tell us that after a divorce, it may be difficult to continue to see their grandchild. Some suggested solutions are:

- If you are in a neutral position with both parents and their homes aren't comfortable for custodial visits, offer your home as a haven for the parents to transfer the grandchildren for scheduled custodial visits.

- If you have no access to your grandchildren for whatever reason, you may need to appeal to the other grandparents or a mutually admired party who may be sympathetic to your plight. If neither of these recourses is successful, you may seek legal recourse to grant visitation rights to be with your grandchildren for a reasonable amount of time. Many states now have laws that allow you to seek a contempt-of-court order against parents who deny visitation rights once those rights have been granted.

Continuity, stability, and loving care are the haven you can give your grandchildren, even while imperma-nence is a fact of life. Therefore, grandparents suggest that you pay close attention to letting your grandchil-dren and children know you love them now.

Don't wait. The love, care, and stability you offer them now will go far to healing the brokenness in their lives.

IN HIS WILL, MY GRANDFATHER (SHOLOM ALEICHEM) STIPULATED, "TAKE CARE OF YOUR GRANDMOTH-ER. PRESERVE YOUR *YIDDISHKEIT*. I

DON'T WANT ANY MONUMENTS. IF
PEOPLE READ MY BOOKS, THAT WILL
BE MY BEST MONUMENT. READ ONE
OF MY STORIES ALOUD IN WHATEVER
LANGUAGE IS CONVENIENT."

Bel Kaufman

Offer Stability in Troubled Times

- On the anniversary of the death of a grandchild, send a card or have prayers said at your church or synagogue.

- Near the birthday of a deceased grandchild contact the parents, offering them a chance to talk and share their feelings about how they would like to spend their child's birthday.

- Gather friends to raise funds for research about the disease or condition that took the life of a grandchild.

- Keep a photograph album of the deceased or absent grandchild.

- Help your child as you are able with carpooling, cleaning, laundry, yard work, gift buying, and the like.

- If the parents of your grandchildren are divorced, implement the strategies named in this chapter so that you can stay in close contact with them.

- If you are separated by distance, communicate via letters, homemade videos, audio tapes, e-mail, websites, and the phone. Save to make a regular visit to see the grandchildren as you are able.

WHERE DID YOU COME FROM BABY DEAR?

OUT OF THE EVERYWHERE INTO THE HERE.

WHERE DID YOU GET YOUR EYES SO BLUE?

OUT OF THE SKY AS I CAME THROUGH.

George McDonald

Angela's Bye-Bye

Every year, a few weeks after the Christmas hubbub has faded away, I set aside an afternoon to do one of my most pleasant tasks. I take out and peruse a gold leather photo album that I began to fill many years ago with family photographs that friends send at the holidays.

The first few years were the young faces of couples standing next to their first Christmas tree or outside their first house or on the ski slope. A few show them holding their first baby. Then came more babies. And more babies. The babies grew, and there were beautiful pictures of weddings on the outside of Christmas greeting cards. It only seemed a blink of an eye, and there were the grandchildren posing with proud grandparents by the Christmas tree or outside of Gran and Gramp's Florida home.

It's like a blessing to arrange those pictures in progression and reminisce about our family and friends. It's amazing to see the Smiths, for example, with thirty-four grandchildren! And the Swansons with quadruplets and two sets of twins in their grandchildren lineup. But one picture always makes me stop for the longest time. It's the picture of a little girl in her long christening gown being held between her adoring grandparents. Her huge China-blue eyes are matched only by her grandmother's eyes of the same color. There's no mistaking who she looks like. It still makes my heart ache to remember that Angela was only here on earth long enough for one Christmas picture.

Angela was the first grandchild of our dear friends John and Helen. Their only daughter Elizabeth and her husband Charles lived in Europe where their careers had taken them and where they had met and married. Helen and John naturally doted on this precious child and took every opportunity to visit the children in Europe, and to show off little Angela to their friends whenever Elizabeth and Charles were home for a visit. There were grandmother tea parties, playtime get-togethers, and every excuse to enjoy their grandchild.

Helen traveled to Belgium a week before Angela's first birthday to help Elizabeth prepare for the big celebration. John wasn't able to leave his job at the time, but Helen promised to take lots of pictures of the big event. The week was filled with happy days and lovely memories. But when it came time for Helen to leave on her flight home, she was reluctant to go because of a nagging feeling that something was wrong with Angela, though a doctor's checkup did not confirm her feelings.

John got the news of Angela's sudden death directly over the phone from a distraught Charles. There had been no way to notify Helen on board her airplane. John walked and prayed all night then went to meet Helen at the airport with the heartbreaking news. Angela had died soon after Helen had left on her flight. Nothing had been able to save her from a virulent form of meningitis.

Helen and John had to find the strength to move through their crushing grief to help Elizabeth and Charles through the agonizing days to come. John recalled, "Somehow, through the grace of God, much prayer, and support from friends and family, we found an inner strength to be there when our daughter needed us. None of us, of course, is the same. We go on, but there is always a hole in our hearts that can't be filled. There have been three beautiful children added to Elizabeth and Charles' family in the five years since Angela left them, and it's a joy to see such a blessing."

John continues to reflect: "I watch Helen hold her newest granddaughter. 'Doesn't she look just like Angela?' she asks, just as I am thinking the very thought. I'm also thinking to myself: Love these babies now, John. Now."

HOW DID YOU COME TO US, YOU DEAR?

GOD THOUGHT ABOUT YOU,

AND SO I AM HERE.

George McDonald

Sidelined

W e are grandparents on "inactive status" these days. I'm sure our story isn't unique, but that really doesn't make us feel any better about what has happened with regard to our grandson.

My husband and I married rather late in life for those days and only had one son, Mark. He was a wonderful child and grew up to be a nice young man. There were a few bumps along the road, but things went along pretty smoothly for our family. Some may even have called us boring and, in relation to what some of our friends and family went through with their kids, I suppose we were.

Mark went to college back East. He majored in engineering and did fine in school. He came home to work every summer. The year he graduated he took off the summer to "bum around" before finding a job. It was during this summer he met his future wife, Jane, while camping at Yellowstone. She was from Phoenix and had a summer job at the National Park. They struck up an instant romance and soon my husband and I were hearing about this wonderful girl. Mark planned to bring Jane home with him at the end of summer to meet us.

My first impression of Jane was that she was a different as night and day from Mark. My husband Tom never really said what his first impression was, but obviously Jane was nowhere as conservative as our son. Her style of dress, her mannerisms, her casual way of immediately addressing Tom and me by our first names was quite different from Mark's past few girlfriends. To be honest it took some getting used to, but Mark was clearly smitten. He was actually more talkative with Jane than I had ever seen him before, and she did have a knack of bringing him out of his shell. After a couple days, Jane's breezy personality got easier to take but there were still some surprises in store.

First, we found out that Jane was a few years older than Mark. Second, and more important, Jane had a two-year-old son living in Phoenix with her parents. This wasn't exactly how we saw our only child starting out his life, but Mark seemed so certain of Jane that we had no choice but to go along with his wishes.

Mark and Jane got an apartment in the city. Mark found his first job with a small technology firm, and they began planning to get married. Jane also found a job, as an administrative assistant in a small theater company. After a couple of months, she started making arrangements for her son to come for a visit from Arizona. I guess the idea was that if Mark and the boy got along well enough then the boy would eventually join his mother.

Tom and I thought it really odd that Mark hadn't even met the little boy before he and Jane took the leap of moving in together, but no one asked our opinion. All we really had heard about this boy were raves from Jane like, "He's the best little baby! My parents have really been so great in helping me out these past few years. The father of my son hasn't ever been in the picture." I tried to get more information from Mark but he didn't know much more than Tom and I did.

The weekend that Jane's son Temple came into our lives stands out as three days of great contrast. First of all, Jane's parents turned out to be a couple not unlike Tom and me. They seemed for all appearances to be normal middle class folks. Besides Jane they had two other children who still lived in Phoenix. From the conversations we had together I learned that Jane was the free spirit of the family. Jane's parents had been helping Jane with Temple since he was born while she was still in college. They had agreed to take Temple full time after Jane graduated so she could have the experience of working at Yellowstone. In retrospect, Jane's set of priorities and this arrangement seem ridiculous.

What to say about Temple? Every grandparent probably feels this way, but Temple really was a special little boy. Initially there were some awkward moments as he readjusted to being with his mother, living with Mark, their marriage, and learning to think of me and Tom as Grandpa and Grandma, but it felt like in no time Temple had always been a part of our lives.

To see Mark with Temple was just a joy. Even though they couldn't have looked less similar, over time Temple began to mimic Mark's way of walking and some of his mannerisms. Strangers always assumed Temple was Mark's son.

We babysat Temple a lot in those early days, which is probably why he warmed up to us to quickly. Being two when he moved here made him at the age of discovery, and we made the most of it. Picnics, the children's museum, the zoo; we showed all of it to Temple. Tom especially loved throwing balls to Temple in the backyard even though it was some time before Temple could throw back with any accuracy. We realized fully what it was like to love a grandson.

Eventually I cut back on my part-time job so I could take care of Temple two days a week. I loved the time Temple and I spent together. I found myself doing things with Temple I had never done with Mark when he was a baby. I even signed him up for early childhood music lessons. Jane seemed to really appreciate what I was doing for her son.

Things went along like that for several years. Tom and I thought we'd stayed close to Mark and Jane throughout, but we were taken aback when we found out Mark and Jane hadn't been getting along. It was as if one day they up and decided they weren't happy. Mark told us they were separating "temporarily" with the hope they'd get back together soon. We continued to take Temple as Jane and Mark decided what they wanted to do.

In the course of things it came out Jane missed the West and didn't think Mark was "exciting enough" for her. I'm sure Mark contributed to their problems, but I can't help thinking Jane was more at fault. The separation dragged on without resolution. Then suddenly, just like that, Jane decided enough was enough, and she wanted to divorce Mark and move back to Phoenix. Mark seemed to give up at that point and let Jane pretty much have her way about everything.

The unfair aspect of the divorce was Jane's decision to take Temple away from Mark. And from us. At that point we were the only family Temple knew. He didn't really know his maternal grandparents anymore and considered Mark his father. Foolishly, Mark never legally adopted Temple and so he didn't have much legal ground to stand on. Jane agreed to let

Mark visit whenever he wanted, but that just isn't the same as living in the same city.

Tom and I were devastated. Just as quickly as Temple had come into our lives, he was being snatched out of it, and we had no power to do anything. It almost felt like we'd lost Temple through death. I felt dumped into a state of grief. I think I still am in it.

We write to Temple and send him presents for his birthday and Christmas, and sometimes he writes to us too. He still says he misses us, but as time goes on and he grows older it is obvious that his memory of us is diminishing. This new notion of mixing families together and then un-mixing them is crazy. I'm sure there are times when it works out well for some families, but it wasn't the case with us. We willingly accepted a little boy and his mother into our lives out of love for our son and made a wonderful family out of our circumstances. And on a whim, it seems, it was all taken away.

So Tom and I still consider ourselves grandparents, just "inactive ones." We hope some day that Temple will want to reconnect with us again, maybe when he's older. We'd certainly welcome that day. Even though our love got us both hurt from the loss, we can still say that we're glad that we took our chances when we had them to love Temple.

Judy Tambornino

LOVE . . . BEARS ALL THINGS, BELIEVES ALL THINGS, HOPES ALL THINGS, ENDURES ALL THINGS. PURSUE LOVE.

Paul of Tarsus

8

It's Okay to Be a Reluctant Grandparent

WHY, WHY WOULD YOU THINK
THAT I WOULD BE HAPPY TO BE A
GRANDMOTHER?

Aurora Greenway in Terms of Endearment

Not everyone is thrilled to become a grandparent. In fact, it's also a myth to believe that everyone just adores little babies.

"I felt like I was just coming into my prime when I first became a grandmother," said one active woman. "I certainly didn't look like the grandmothers I knew when I was growing up. I still had my looks. People often mistook me for my daughter's friend or sister, not her mother. I was proud of that. I was still active in my profession, played golf nearly every day, and had recently taken up tennis and rollerblading. I just wasn't ready to be relegated into the grandmother category."

Her daughter continued the conversation with us, saying, "Mother always says she'd like to baby-sit little Colin, but when we call, she's never there! She and Dad are always out somewhere. I thought they'd slow down but they're more active than they were when I was growing up. Sometimes I think they're just avoiding us!"

Another grandmother added, "I was so young when I had my own children, and I was only forty when my oldest daughter got pregnant. I calculated that would mean that I would spend thirty-five to forty years with babies and children underfoot. I just wasn't ready to accept that."

And another commented, "My daughter-in-law and I have a strained relationship. She naturally pines for her own mother, but it's more than that. She has been, at times, really hostile to me. So it was hard to get excited about her pregnancy even though the baby was also my son's first child."

Grandfathers have hesitations, too. One granddad told us: "Our house has just gotten quiet and orderly. My wife and I are looking forward to enjoying our leisure years. I have to be frank. Babies scream and cry a lot. They have this terrible habit of throwing up and drooling all over my clean clothes, and when they're older they race around the house and destroy what they don't disrupt: which is my sanity!"

Another grandfather said, "My infant grandson cries and stiffens every time I try to pick him up. Face it, I was on the road so much when my kids were little, I didn't develop the knack of relating to small babies. I really only enjoy them when they've been housebroken and can carry on a decent conversation."

One grandfather we know set the tone for his relationship with his grandchildren when he came to the hospital to view his first grandson in the newborn nursery. "He looks like a squashed prune!" he said. Even today, eight grandchildren later, he spends his golden years traveling as much as he can and says he'd rather enjoy the grandchildren from the "safe distance of a homemade video screening or computer generated e-mail message."

It's true that many grandfathers feel uncomfortable around babies and young children. They may not have known their own grandfathers since it's only been recently that the life expectancy of men has risen into the seventies. Similarly, many of these men were not nurtured by their fathers either, and therefore have no models of how to be comfortable with their grandchildren.

The baby boom generation may break any pattern of non-engagement with grandchildren. Theirs is a generation of men who have been encouraged to express their emotions, particularly their nurturing, caring natures.

This may be a new era for grandmothers as well. Women have been supported in fulfilling dreams of further education, self-expression, and leadership as never before. After her children are reared, a mature woman may decide to return to a university to complete her education, pursue creative expression, open a business, run for office, or volunteer for the Peace Corps. This means that families will need to openly share any expectations parents and grandparents might have for each other. There may even be some old baggage both parties may need to air in order to clear a path to a harmonious working relationship.

Even if you don't want your grandchildren around all the time and you don't like diapers and drool, you still have gifts to offer and are important in their lives. In particular, as described before, you offer your wisdom, the synthesis of experience and continued new learning. Some reluctance and even nervousness about grandparenting is understandable, so ponder its meaning for you—what you bring to your grandchildren and what they bring to you.

ACCEPTANCE OF ONE'S LIFE HAS NOTHING TO DO WITH RESIGNATION; IT DOES NOT MEAN RUNNING

AWAY FROM THE STRUGGLE. ON THE
CONTRARY, IT MEANS ACCEPTING IT
AS IT COMES, WITH ALL THE HANDI-
CAPS OF HEREDITY, OF SUFFERING,
OF PSYCHOLOGICAL COMPLEXITIES
AND INJUSTICES.

Paul Tournier

It's Okay to Be a Reluctant Grandparent

- Assess what you can and cannot do for your grandchildren, taking into consideration your physical,
emotional, and spiritual resources and abilities.
Communicate your reflections to the parents of your
grandchildren.

- Enroll in a course or program for physical fitness.
Caring for a small child—even for a very short
time—is taxing. For example, if you plan to do regular baby-sitting, you may need to build upper body
strength so you can lift the fairly heavy car seats
now required by law for every small child.

- Be honest about your limitations and give yourself
permission to say no to too many expectations. List
the things that you will or will not do for your grandchildren. Be sure that you give each careful discernment and feel comfortable with each commitment.

GRANDMOTHERS ARE EITHER
LONELY OR TIRED.

Anne Morrow Lindbergh

Unexpected Crisis

Maureen was looking forward to the day that she had planned with her two darling grandchildren, Connor, age three, and Meghan, age eighteen months. It was a sunny May morning, and she was already feeling energized after her yoga and one tall skim post-workout latte from the Starbucks "drive-thru."

She would take them on a walk around the lake near the park, sail paper boats, feed the ducks, and then head to the zoo with its merry-go-round. A picnic would conclude the time before their nap. Maureen was just loading two CDs into the disk player in her brand new SUV when her son, Tom, pulled into the driveway to drop off Meghan and Connor. Tom was giving her his check list of "do's and don'ts " for the children when Lucy, the six-year-old neighbor girl, came over to see her favorite little friend, Meghan. "Let me read to Meghan for a minute while you get Connor into his car seat," Lucy said. "That's a big help, Lucy," Maureen replied as she lifted Connor into his place.

Maureen was beginning to wonder if it might not be turning into too warm a day for all the activities she had planned as she wiped the perspiration from off her upper lip. "Oh, Lucy, I think we're ready to go so you'd better jump out of the car now," Maureen said as she turned to pick up the picnic basket to place it in the back of the SUV.

Lucy, always the little helper, jumped out of the back seat and promptly shut the door, which simultaneously set the automatic door locks into the "lock" position even though the keys were still in the ignition. It happened in an instant. Maureen could only stand in the driveway frozen in disbelief. A slow knot of anxiety began to grow in her stomach. Then she recovered herself.

"Don't panic, Maureen," she muttered to herself. "You have another set of keys in your purse which," she heard her thoughts climb into a screech, "is sitting on the front seat of the car!"

By now she seemed to be shouting to herself, "Don't panic, get Connor to unlock the front door!" Maureen flattened her face against the hot front passenger seat window where Connor was sitting. "Connor, please unbuckle your seat belt so you can reach over and pull up the lock on the door, honey." Maureen struggled to keep the panic out of her voice.

Connor shook his red curls, "No!" He would not be persuaded to unbuckle his seat belt and get out of the car seat his daddy had buckled him into. (Connor had heard his mommy saying many times over, "*Never* unbuckle your seat belt.") Nothing Maureen said—not pleading, not threats, nor telling Connor he would be a *hero*—moved him from his position in the car seat.

Now Maureen was in full panic. Her heart pounded, her throat was dry, she felt nauseous. She looked in the back seat. Meghan's fair skin was turning a dark pink.

Desperate, Maureen ran into the house and called 911. She explained to the operator, "No, I don't have an extra set of keys, and no, I don't know how to break into my own car!"

Running out to the SUV to plead with Connor again, she heard the siren of a police car as it rounded the corner followed by, not one, but two fire engines with their lights flashing.

The first two firefighters on the scene couldn't seem to spring the car locks. Meghan's skin was literally turning red. One firefighter declared, "Lady, I think we're going to have to break your car window to get in."

Maureen couldn't believe the thought that escaped out of her lips, "I'd rather you gentlemen didn't!"

But they didn't roll their eyes, and they didn't hesitate. A burly firefighter picked up a hammer with his gloved hand and shattered the driver's side window, the one farthest away from the children. They gently removed the children from their car seats, Connor still protesting that he didn't want to disobey his mommy, while simultaneously showing with his twinkling blue eyes and animated gestures he was really excited about being the center of all this attention from the firefighters and police officers.

As Maureen looked around, she saw one of the other police officers pick up Meghan and carefully lay her down on the grass, while the firefighters gently cooled the children down with a spray of cool water, first Meghan, then Connor. Both children seemed impressed.

Maureen was not consoled. The firefighters, and police were giving her sidelong glances, clearly signaling that they thought she was too old and probably inept to care for small children. She could just see a newspaper headline: "Local Grandma Arrested for Child Endangerment."

At last police officers, firefighters, and neighbors dispersed. Maureen abandoned her plans for a perfect day at the park. She took Connor and Meghan into the house to calm them down, dry them off, and feed them their picnic lunch in the air conditioned house. With orders to Connor "not to move from the couch," Maureen called her son Tom to come pick up his children early.

Connor obeyed his grandmother, not moving from the couch where she'd placed him. When Maureen returned she saw him having a perfectly wonderful time printing his name with a sharp pen on Maureen's new white leather couch.

When Tom pulled up to reclaim the darling grandchildren, Maureen caught sight of herself in the hall mirror. Her eyes had the glazed look of someone who'd gone for days without sleep, her hair was matted with sweat, her clothes were wrinkled, and she knew, in that moment, she was definitely old enough to be a grandmother.

Over the river and through the woods
to grandmother's house we go
When we got there, the cupboard was bare
with a note saying
"We've gone to the Florida condo!"

Margaret Cousineau

Not Your Cozy Grandmother

I'm not the warm, cozy grandmother of lore whose door is always open to her grandchildren; who always has freshly baked Toll House cookies and hot cocoa ready for them as they visit her and tell her their inmost thoughts and soak up her wisdom. Heavens, I wasn't even a good mother!

After my divorce, I finished raising my children and then returned to graduate school. My degree was in statistical analysis and geopolitics. It was an emerging area at the time and I became the state's first demographer, advising legislators about economic growth and populations changes. But when it comes to my relationship with my grandkids, well, I'm a classic eccentric, quite odd! This story will tell you how so.

Three years ago, I arranged, as I always did, to have everyone over for Christmas Eve. Now, I'd always enjoyed decorating the house, trimming the tree, and cooking a festive meal. I'd rather looked forward to the evening. I'd imagined we'd open Christmas presents by the fire, sing carols, and read *A Christmas Carol*.

I should have gotten a hint of what was to come when I opened my front door to let my son-in-law, Anthony, daughter, Amelia, and their two girls, Tiffany and Sophia, into my apartment. The little girls had the look of two drinks of sour milk. Anthony's face was pinched. Amelia gave me an air kiss, then crossed the living room floor and set up a DVD player. The girls followed her and immediately turned up the volume of this cacophonous metal sound they've apparently grown fond of.

I fled to the kitchen for shelter and solace. Why didn't I see this coming? Why did I think we'd have an old-fashioned Christmas with songs and stories? After all, during our last two visits, Amelia was put out with me because I refused to abandon my post in the kitchen and sit and watch a boring DVD movie with the girls. So, I did it again. I hid in the kitchen until supper was ready.

We ate my cordon bleu meal in silence until the girls, who were hunched down, sulking and poking at their meal, started fighting. I don't remember what it was about, but it ended dramatically with spilled milk and smashed glass all over my linen tablecloth. Amelia's response was to gather up the little monsters and hiss at me that if I weren't so x@#%* uptight and showed a little interest in my grandchildren that life would be ever so much more pleasant.

Anthony chimed in something to the effect, "Come on girls, your grandmother may own the world, but God owns your souls."

I could barely hold back my tears of hurt and fury as they swept out of my apartment. When I turned and caught sight of the dining room in disarray and the unopened presents under the tree, I sat down and sobbed.

Christmas morning, I came to my senses. I realized I needed to first take care of myself if I was to get on with life. So, I wrote letters to both my children. I wrote that I didn't want to have any more contact with them. I loved them. Therefore, I wanted, from this day forward, to eliminate any situation that would likely lead to contention.

This was a dramatic and shocking decision, I admit. But what's really shocking to me is what happens to grandmothers all over this country nowadays. In other countries when a mother rears her family and then has grandchildren, her status is elevated. She has weathered many difficulties in bringing her children to maturity. As grandmother, her grandchildren, her children, and the community revere her, and value her wisdom, experience, and memory of cultural life. Without her, the life of the community could not go on. But here—and my family is no different—as a grandmother, as an older woman alone, I have no status. I am in the way. I am a crashing bore to my family.

But I can't change our country's mores. As a demographer, I can only analyze facts and statistics. I knew in that moment of epiphany, I had to take care of myself. I couldn't control what my children did or thought. So I made a list of the things I love and want to do. I read and make tapes for the Braille Society so blind children can discover the pleasure of books. I myself read until 3 a.m. if I want to and sleep in late. And, I always wanted to do two things: paint with watercolor and fly an airplane. So, I did both. I joined a watercolor class and just love it. Flying was definitely more challenging and more rewarding. I qualified as a pilot, then qualified to pilot a glider.

Last Christmas, instead of moping around, I went to Antigua, Guatemala, with two of my friends. We also volunteered at a mission near there—San Lucas Toleman. It was the most meaningful Christmas of my whole life. I felt more alive than I have in years.

And, yes, in case you're wondering, the relationship with my grandchildren is being repaired, slowly but surely.

The silence was broken when the elder of my grandchildren, Tiffany, called me and asked if we could meet sometime for lunch. I hesitated because I thought this might be a setup engineered by her mother, but something nudged me forward and I said, "Yes, I'd like that very much."

We had lunch, the first of many, at Tiffany's favorite spot, an inn popular with kids her age. We talked until the inn closed for the evening crowd. I found her to be delightful. Part of the reason was, and is, that we have the same interests. We talked about world affairs, history, the possibility of peace in her lifetime and quantum physics.

Since that time, I try to get together with each grandchild alone at a place of her choosing, but still neutral ground if you will. We've also arranged some "group outings" with more of the grandkids together when we go to a museum, play, or movie.

I've found out that my grandkids are able to converse on so many subjects. I learn so much when I'm with them. As for their parents, it's tacit agreement that they not interfere with this arrangement. Heaven help them if they did!

Then just last week Jonathan, my youngest grandchild, called me and asked me to come with him to his school. It was an unusual request but I agreed. I was curious. When I got there, I was amazed to see the schoolroom filled with hamsters, ferrets, painted turtles, dolls, and complex Lego constructions. Besides the teacher, a Mrs. Gonzales, I was the only adult in the room.

Mrs. Gonzales came up to me, took both my hands and said, "Oh, I've been so eager to meet you; Jonathan talks about you all the time. Today the children were asked to bring their favorite thing to class and tell us about it. You are Jonathan's favorite thing!"

When "show and tell" began, Jonathan took my hand. He told his classmates that I was his hero because even though I was a grandma, I flew planes and gliders, and read to children who can't see. "And she helps people in far away places harvest coffee beans. Best of all, I get to go places with Grandma and learn about the world, 'cause Grandma's really smart and teaches us a lot." He squeezed my hand and through my misted glasses I could see every face turned to me in rapt admiration.

ONE HOUR WITH A CHILD IS LIKE A

TEN-MILE RUN.

Joan Benoit Samuelson

9

Learn to Cherish Special Blessings

WE ARE THE SPECIES THAT TAKE
CARE OF CHILDREN.

Melvin Konner

In many African villages instead of greeting one
another with, "How are you?" they ask, "How are the
children?" After all, if the children are well, the whole
village is well and there is nothing to worry about.

How the children *are* depends a lot on the ones
answering the question, especially if the children have
special needs or challenges or chronic illnesses. Sadly,
some grandparents never adapt to and accept the special needs of their grandchildren. Happily, most grandparents discover that children with special needs also
bring special blessings.

Two friends represent that fact for us.

Marilyn and I were catching up on each other's family news one Sunday afternoon. I asked her about her
granddaughter Sarah, who was born with Down syndrome. Marilyn always beamed with pride when she
related each new accomplishment in Sarah's development. Her pride in her son Steve and her daughter-in-
law Gail, Sarah's parents, could fill volumes. "The way

they are raising Sarah allows her to fit into the family beautifully. She is no different from any of the other grandchildren." Sarah's story—shared on pages 106-109—shows how true this is.

Matthew is the grandson of our friends Peggy and Bob. Matthew is also a cousin of one of Priscilla's former religious education students. At age eighteen months, Matthew, a happy, bright, active little boy contracted virulent septicemia and almost died. Matthew's story (pages 109-112) is one of courage, love, and a deep, abiding faith.

"How is your grandchild?" This is a question that grandparents are usually most pleased to answer. Grandparents of children with special needs are no different. Of course we wish that each child have perfect health and the full range of human talents and abilities. Of course a certain amount of emotional and spiritual adjustment is required. These adjustments should not be minimized.

Nevertheless, grandparents of children with special challenges can respond to "How is your grandchild?" with either somber vagueness or sad complaints or they can also answer, "Wonderful! Miraculous!" and then launch into glowing and typical grandparent stories.

EVERYTHING THAT HAPPENS IS EITHER A BLESSING WHICH IS ALSO A LESSON, OR A LESSON WHICH IS ALSO A BLESSING.

Polly Berrien Berends

Learn to Cherish Special Blessings

- Grandparents of children who are special make these suggestions, so consider each one and how it might fit for you:
    - Provide extra love and support, in whatever way you can: Baby-sit or take over for the parents for a weekend so they can get needed rest.
    - Find out all you can about the special needs of your grandchild and draw on your spiritual and emotional reserves to encourage a positive response to your children as well as your new grandchild.
    - Contact other grandparents of children with special needs and participate with them in a support group.
    - Find out what you can about special clinics: for example, speech and hearing, therapeutic play including equestrian therapy, warm water swimming, and aerobics. If possible, make going to these clinics a special time for you and your special grandchild.
- Set aside some time each day to remind yourself of the blessings that come to you from your special grandchild.
- Do not neglect the other children the family. Often the best thing you can do for the parents is care for and play with the other children.

THE UNAWAKENED MIND TENDS TO MAKE

WAR AGAINST THE WAY THINGS ARE.

Jack Kornfield

That Your Love May Increase

Advent, the season before Christmas, is one of waiting and hope. This anticipation builds to a wonderful climax of the birth of the baby Jesus. Advent is also a time of great beauty and peace.

As a mother of small children, I associate Advent with the theme of pregnancy and of the hope and anticipation and earnest love a mother has in expectation of a pending birth. As Mary the mother of Jesus knew, while carrying a child is a physical challenge, it is an emotional and spiritual joy.

My husband and I have five children in our family. It is Sarah, our youngest child at just over one year old, who has been a symbol of my own personal advent. When my husband and I learned that we were expecting our fifth child, we were simply overjoyed. My previous pregnancy had ended in a miscarriage and so this pregnancy promised healing for both of us.

Because of my age, and because of some early blood tests, we chose to have additional testing done that looked more closely for chromosomal disorders, and specifically Down syndrome.

Technology is a miraculous thing in our society today. It gives us so much information, so quickly and in such detail, that we have all learned to trust and rely on it. And so it was with a sigh of relief that the specialist told us that he could detect no abnormalities and that we could be certain that our child was healthy and normal.

Unfortunately, in leaving the office that day, I knew he was wrong and that my child had Down syndrome. I can't tell you how I knew. But I did. And it filled me with fear. Although I couldn't bring myself to tell my husband or my doctor at that point, I did begin to pray.

As I reached my last month, I felt more and more sure that my child would not be "typical." And then, something unusual and extraordinary happened, and I have to admit to you today, it takes courage for me to share it with you.

One week before Sarah was born, I found myself returning from a luncheon with one of my husband's relatives. We had a thirty-minute car ride ahead of us, and she began to talk with me about her life growing up with a younger brother who had Down syndrome.

I had been having labor pains that afternoon, so I was silent and a bit uncomfortable, but she didn't seem to notice my cues and just kept on talking. In that thirty-minute period she told me everything that I needed to know about Down syndrome.

She told me that a person with Down syndrome has an extra twenty-first chromosome. She told me that Down syndrome could come with other serious health problems. She told me that people with Down syndrome have very wide ranges of mental capabilities and that while it did mean mental retardation, it did not mean social retardation. She also shared her extreme gratitude and thankfulness that her family was chosen to have this special child and that it was an incredibly positive experience. She told me, "Gail, my brother is a gift from God."

When I got out of the car, she drove away. I stood in the parking lot of the grocery store I was going to and said out loud, "I hear you God!" And I did hear him. I believe that he had sent me a messenger to warn and prepare me.

When we were driving to the hospital to deliver Sarah, I turned to my husband and said, "Are you ready for a child with Down syndrome?" His reply, thank God, was, "Yes, we can handle anything that happens."

She was born at midnight. And although she was healthy, she didn't have the strength to cry. She was strangely limp and silent. And she was beautiful.

My doctor left the room because, he told me later, he wasn't sure how to break the news. I remember telling him and my husband and the nurse, "She is our gift from God." But I really didn't understand what that meant.

In the Bible, when Mary first learned that she was pregnant with Jesus, her reply was, "I am the servant of the Lord. Let it be done unto me as you say." I wish I could stand before you and say that was my reaction when Sarah was born. But I cannot.

When my husband left me that night to return to our other children, I sat alone in my hospital bed and that was my darkest hour. I prayed for God to remove this extra chromosome and to give me my "real daughter." I begged him, "Anything but this!"

But when I awoke that morning, I heard six or seven babies crying in the hallway as the nurses were delivering them to their mothers for feeding. And I could pick out my daughter's cry from all the rest, even though it was the first time I had heard her voice. When I held her, I knew complete peace, and my heart began to heal.

Those first few months of her life were surreal. Some people responded well to the news, but most people wept. I received sympathy messages from people instead of congratulations. Most people stayed away because they weren't sure what to say. My church congregation was wonderful, I must say. I remember my husband saying, "Honey, I'm really looking forward to bringing Sarah to the basilica. I just know that she will be welcomed there." And she was.

My family has come a long way since then. Sarah has filled our home with grace and love. And any fear or hesitation we had was just washed away. It was and it continues to be very difficult to feel anything but happiness being with her. And the fear and dread I felt was replaced by a very peaceful love and strong pride in being chosen her mother. In short, she is our great gift from God.

That is a resounding theme you will hear from families with special-needs kids. There is a peace and joy that is hard to explain. While other people may unwittingly feel pity towards us, they have grossly misjudged the experience. I think often of the words of a beautiful prayer:

That your love may increase ever more and more

In the knowledge and every kind of perception

To discern what is of value.

Gail Dorn-Beddor

YOU [GOD] KNIT ME IN MY MOTHER'S WOMB. I PRAISE YOU, FOR I AM FEARFULLY AND WONDERFULLY MADE.

Psalm 139

Changed Forever

One of the biggest benefits in being a grandparent is having time to relate to and enjoy our grandchildren. No more diapers to change, homework to monitor, or kids to ready for school and church. We have enjoyed our grandchildren on leisurely visits. Then we say goodbye.

We were especially happy and involved with our first grandchild, Matthew. He was a beautiful child with his grandpa's and his father's red hair and his own lovely hazel eyes. He was bright and humorous.

He and Grandpa would play with his toys, or he would help me and his mom cook in the kitchen.

Often it is difficult to put into words an incident that has entered your life, changed it, and will be there forever. It is not always easy to open doors that have been closed for a long time because you begin to relive your experiences. We find this true when we talk about Matthew.

When Matthew was eighteen months old, he contracted a virulent septicemia and almost died. We did not find out until later that he had no spleen, which could have helped him ward off this infection.

Nothing prepared us for the frightening phone call from his mom one morning. Matthew had had a cold but awoke that morning with a high fever, so high that his mom, Cheri, called 911. Cheri then called his father, Andrew, who was in his fourth year surgical residency at Hennepin County Medical Center.

Andrew met the ambulance when it arrived at Children's Hospital. After a cursory examination, he realized his son was close to death. He had alerted the ER at the hospital, and the doctors put Matthew on a respirator, blood pressure medications, antibiotics, and incubated him within a very short time in an attempt to stabilize him.

Andrew and his colleagues called all over the country, talking to doctors who had some knowledge of the disease. The news was not good. Collectively the doctors had seen only fourteen cases: twelve had died, and the two that lived had brain damage.

The doctors at Children's Hospital worked around the clock and gradually Matthew's fever lessened. They felt that his brain had been spared, but the blood had clotted and there was no circulation in his extremities. After several days on anticoagulants and several trips to the hyperbaric chamber, it was apparent that the circulation in his arms and legs was permanently damaged. The doctors had done their very best, but even that was not enough.

The doctors all agreed that he needed surgery before gangrene set in. So, on that difficult day, they removed Matthew's arms above his elbows and his legs above his knees. Needless to say, our family was devastated.

After the amputations, Matthew was moved to Hennepin County Burn Unit for grafts. He was there for over two months. Matthew's stay at Hennepin was as good as any hospital stay could be. Cheri, who is so wonderful and efficient, saw that everything was done as it should be. A family member was there with Matthew all night, every night Matthew was in the hospital.

One night Andrew and Cheri were standing by his crib and a ceiling light was shining on Matthew. Unexpectedly, he opened his eyes, looking directly at his parents, and then closed them and went to sleep. They thought of this as a sign from God that he would be all right.

After his stay at Hennepin, Matthew went to another facility for a month and worked with the therapists there. It was then we realized that even if you have physical limitations, you can accomplish so many wonderful things.

Four of my six children were near home when Matthew first became ill. All, at one time or another, contributed generously to the support and help of Andrew and Cheri. My youngest daughter is a free-lance writer and had more time to devote to Matthew. She took him in his wheelchair on what she called "adventures." They traveled the hospital using the elevators, went to the park, and even sat and watched the cars go by. She had projects for him and read to him often and, to this day, she is still his mentor and one of his dearest friends.

Andrew has said that one must be candid and realize there are many bumps along the road. There are instances when Matthew has to go back to the hospital to have some work done on his extremities. Each trip is very difficult for him. Andrew and Cheri have a personal caretaker at their home continuously. Besides Matthew, they also have two other children who require love, care, and attention.

We try to continue our support by going to many of the children's functions. We went to Matthew's baseball games and to watch him ski this winter, which is his favorite sport. He sits on a tethered chair and goes lickety-split down the hill with a person tethering the ropes.

Andrew and Cheri make a great point of spending time teaching and encouraging their children to love God and read the Bible. They have taught Matthew self-love and esteem. He is a pro at the computer and can go almost anywhere in his wheelchair. Matthew has all his badges as a Boy Scout and will begin his Sea Scout work next year. He is an excellent student and has spoken to the Minnesota Senate about assistance needed for the handicapped and offered testimony about the Shriners who helped him in their hospital. He is on the debate team at his school and, most importantly, has many wonderful friends.

We believe our family has handled Matthew's tragic illness well. It brought our family closer together and hopefully has made us more compassionate and loving human beings. We could not be more proud of Matthew. He is not our special needs grandchild. He is our special blessing. And we believe God continues to have a special plan for him.

Peggy and Bob Fink

ON OUR EARTHLY SOJOURN, WAIT-
ING IS LONG AND THE DARKNESS
CAN BE TERRIFYING. BUT WHEN
GOD'S SPIRIT INFLAMES OUR SOUL
WITH LOVE, THEN THE WILDERNESS
AND OUR SOUL REJOICE.

Robert Morneau

1 0

You Don't Always Have to Like Your Kids' Spouses

IT'S AN ETERNAL MYSTERY HOW THE
BOY WHO WASN'T GOOD ENOUGH
TO MARRY YOUR DAUGHTER IS THE
FATHER OF THE MOST BRILLIANT
GRANDCHILD IN THE WORLD.

Jewish Folk Saying

For the sake of our grandkids, let's admit frankly that we might not like one of our sons- or daughters-in-law. It's important to be clear about the fact that you dread seeing them come through the door and about the reasons why. It's necessary to be honest in this area unless you want to pay the price of losing a relationship with not only your child, but your grandchildren as well.

For most of us, the price is too high to pay. So we hide our feelings only to be surprised when they ooze out in the most unexpected ways and at the most inconvenient times. To avoid this, it's important to tell the truth to ourselves, for sure, and to a trusted confidant besides. Between you and your friend or counselor, you can sift the chaff from the wheat and develop a clear plan for living with your family in harmony.

In exploring the terrain of dislike you may want to look into the ruts of prejudice worn deep into the ground by generations before you. You might look at the sudden changes that you or your spouse may not have been prepared for or that you want to resist. Another undulation to explore might be fear and anxiety over loss of dreams or achievements that your child's marriage and subsequently your grandchild might represent.

And, you might want to explore your own shadows. Shadows represent personality traits that are in the deep recesses of our souls because either we or our family fear and despise them. What we despise in others is often what we most fear in ourselves. These are our shadows. When we spot these hated traits in another, we judge that person harshly, avoid them, or marginalize them.

Finally, there may be unfinished aspects of the relationship between you and your son or daughter that you have never felt free to communicate. If so, these may affect your relationship with your son-in-law or daughter-in-law.

In our family, so the legend goes, my maternal grandmother had fantasies about her daughters marrying men of wealth and social stature. Only one of the four actually did. My mother was not the one. My father had several marks against him as a suitable son-in-law. First and foremost, he was not Roman Catholic, the family religion. His parents were devout Methodists. Second, he was poor. Third, he hadn't finished college. Finally—and this may have been the seat of her dislike— my father's maternal aunt, the only relative my grandparents knew, was the nastiest woman in town. "What good," my grandmother asked, "could come out of a family who had produced a witch like that?"

Nevertheless, in time, my father proved to be her favorite son-in-law. The ice started to melt between them upon the arrival of our oldest sister, Betty, their first grandchild.

Needless to say, if you either intuitively or concretely know that your child and grandchild are in danger of harm from the abusive or cruel behavior of your child's spouse, you're duty-bound to intervene for their protection, with the assistance of legal and counseling professionals. Similarly, if your son or daughter-in-law is hell-bent on stirring up trouble and dissension in your family, it's necessary to address that behavior forthrightly.

Just as it's said that "old age is not for sissies," the same could be said for grandparenting. It takes courage to make an honest assessment of ourselves, level old prejudices, let go of fantasies about what might have been, and relax and enjoy the new family that grandchildren help to form.

IT MAY BE THAT THE MOST DIFFICULT CHALLENGE IS WHETHER YOU CAN AFFORD TO BE INFLEXIBLE.

Eda LeShan

You Don't Always Have to Like Your Kids' Spouses

- Consider your history with your child's spouse that you don't particularly like. Describe a few of the things about him or her that most annoy or disturb you. Try to tie each annoyance to a particular example of the behavior. Next to each example, recall and describe how you reacted and any results of your reactions. Honestly write a brief summary of your tense relationship. Get it all out in front of you on paper.

- List all the positive attributes and behaviors of this son- or daughter-in-law. Clearly your daughter or son saw good traits in this person. Try to put some of your annoyance away and list the positives.

- Knowing that you do not have the power or responsibility to change this in-law, what is the best possible relationship you can hope to have with this person? Name many possible positive scenarios.

- Ponder these questions and try to strategize about answers: How can I encourage and support what is positive about my child's spouse? How can I let go of my own behaviors that cause tension between us?

- In all cases, you might find solace and courage praying the Serenity Prayer: "God grant me serenity to accept the things I cannot change, courage to change the things I can, and wisdom to know the difference."

THOUGHTS ARE LIKE ARROWS:

ONCE RELEASED, THEY STRIKE THEIR

MARK.

GUARD THEM WELL OR ONE DAY

YOU MAY BE YOUR OWN VICTIM.

Navajo Proverb

For the Sake of the Grandkids

There are times when I can't stand to be around my son-in-law, Billy. In my opinion, he's lazy. His laziness is in direct proportion to his size: huge. Billy weighs about 360 pounds, very heavy even for a person of 6'3". He orders his shoes from a specialty store that sells to NBA and NFL behemoths. I guess I ought to feel sorry for him, and I probably would if he weren't married to my daughter and father to my two grandsons.

Billy's family of origin defines dysfunctional. His father is temporarily living in the sorry state of bachelorhood after his fifth wife took off with a man her own age: that is, thirty years younger than Billy's pappy. Billy's mother is on husband number four, but this one may work out because she's in her sixties and not likely to snag another husband as rich as the lawyer she's got. Billy has, at last count, about ten half-siblings scattered among the various combinations of ex-stepmothers and ex-stepfathers. And of course, Billy's father and mother are at each other like pit bulls, too often with Billy getting mangled in the middle.

Now don't get me wrong. My wife and I aren't perfect and neither is our family. But our clan is an island of stability compared with the hurricane-lashed sea of Billy's bunch. But as I was saying, Billy tries a person's tolerance for ineptitude and sloth. Sure, his obesity makes it difficult for him to breathe, so he suffers from sleep apnea so bad that he had to have surgery to try to fix it. He's tried dieting, but cannot find one diet that includes Southern fried chicken, deep fried catfish, french fries, potato salad, honey-cured ham, and corn bread made with lard.

Billy did finish high school and has a couple of semesters of junior college under his size 60 belt. But, without receiving any encouragement or help from his family, he decided to drop out of college before getting a degree. Besides, his father lured him away from school with promises of a job with his "advertising" company. I hesitate to call it an advertising company because what they really sold were garish billboards that gave roadside trash a good name. Anyway, after a few months, Billy found out that all of his father's promises of big money vanished like his daddy's ever-skyward cigarette smoke.

When his dreams of becoming an ad executive evaporated, Billy looked to law enforcement. So now Billy is a deputy sheriff, wearing a mean-looking gun, a shiny badge, and handcuffs as he patrols the County Building and environs looking for vagrants, illegal parkers, and other such miscreants. I'll give it to him, he seems to do a pretty good job of it, despite his hope-lessly flat feet and shambling gait. As long as he does not have to run after anyone more nimble than your octogenarian auntie, he's your man. Having to be on patrol all day leaves Billy incapable of doing any more when he arrives home than crashing in front of the TV and falling into fitful slumber as reruns of *Mr. Ed* flash on the screen.

I know that I sound harsh, but his ineptitude and laziness mean that my daughter has to be mother and father to the kids. That I resent—for her and for us. My daughter teaches in school all day. Indeed, she's the pri-mary breadwinner. To help pay the bills that Billy's accrued because of his regular illnesses and paying off two pickup trucks Billy wrecked when he fell asleep at the wheel, she also tutors adults trying to learn Spanish.

I had gotten so hardhearted towards Billy that my daughter didn't like to talk to me about him or even the kids. This was the time, thankfully, I found reasons to think better of my son-in-law. It was also the time my mother-in-law, Virginia, began to alternate between a state of fiery crankiness and mellow sweetness. As her health declined, she was falling more often, hurting herself, becoming steadily more forgetful, and causing Jane and I constant worry. More importantly, she needed something to look forward to. She had been desperately lonely ever since my father-in-law died.

Then, all of a sudden, my wife Jane and I noticed a gradual new alertness in Virginia. While she still moved hesitantly and didn't remember things too well, she had just a bit more sparkle in her eyes. She also had started asking us to buy more chocolate chip cookies and milk when we shopped for her. Why we didn't ask about this sudden interest in cookies and milk I can't answer. In any case, we were just pleased in her new brightness.

A couple of weeks after we had seen Virginia looking better, I happened by her apartment earlier in the afternoon than usual. When I pulled into the lot, I noticed Billy's pickup. Walking to her door, I noticed that it was open and heard adult laughter and children's giggles coming from inside. Wondering what this was about, I peeked inside.

Huddled in her tiny breakfast nook were Billy, my two grandsons sharing the same chair, and Virginia. The four of them were dipping their chocolate chip cookies in glasses of milk and then chorusing in unison, "In the mouth before the cookie crumbles." Quickly they'd stuff the drenched cookies into their mouths while they giggled. Virginia's eyes danced. The boys—including Billy—seemed never to have had so much fun.

Rather than break that circle of joy, I backed away with my sour attitude towards Billy. I drove home delighted to see Virginia so happy. While telling Jane about the good times around Virginia's table, I had to wonder if indeed there weren't other positive qualities in Billy that I had overlooked. In a fit of soul-searching, I did a quick inventory, trying to uncover things I could affirm in him so that I could be more positive. Being sour on Billy wasn't doing any of us much good, especially the grandkids.

I do remember this conversation I had with a fellow member of my church. He had told me, "When you see Billy, thank him again for helping my wife change her tire yesterday."

"You mean my son-in-law Billy?" I asked him.

"Sure. He's really a good guy." I couldn't believe that this was the same Billy.

Once I started looking for signs of goodness, I kept finding them, sort of like when you buy a new car you start noticing that—much to your amazement—lots of other folks have that same brand. I'm now trying to do things with my grandkids that I know Billy won't or can't. I take them fishing, and we've even gone camping a couple of times, though my fifty-something back may not take much more of that. When they're a bit older I'll teach them about cutting the lawn and planting flowers.

Don't get me wrong, I still get ticked off at Billy. I'm not his greatest fan. But I'm trying to change my attitude towards Billy. I had better—for my daughter Sandra's sake and for my two grandsons.

An old Jew and a young Jew are traveling on the train. The young Jew asks: "Excuse me, what time is it?" The old Jew does not answer. "Excuse me, sir, what time is it?" The old Jew keeps silent. "Sir, I'm asking you what time is it. Why don't you answer?" The old Jew says,

"SON, THE NEXT STOP IS THE LAST
ON THIS ROUTE. I DON'T KNOW
YOU, SO YOU MUST BE A STRANGER.
IF I ANSWER YOU NOW, I'LL HAVE TO
INVITE YOU TO MY HOME. YOU'RE
HANDSOME, AND I HAVE A BEAUTI-
FUL DAUGHTER. YOU WILL BOTH
FALL IN LOVE AND YOU WILL WANT
TO GET MARRIED. TELL ME, WHY
WOULD I NEED A SON-IN-LAW WHO
CAN'T EVEN AFFORD A WATCH?"

from the Big Little Book of
Jewish Wit and Wisdom

Merry Christmas! Right?

Hurrying into the restaurant, Diana slid into the chair across from Mary. "Gee, it's good to see you. I've got to talk." Tapping her fingernails sharply on the hard tabletop, like a hawk looking for a prairie dog, Diana's eyes darted around for someone to take her order.

"Are you jumpy or what? Okay, sweetie, what's up?" asked Mary.

"I need to vent to someone and, as my dear old friend, you're the lucky one."

"Oh, boy!" Mary was already halfway into her jumbo-sized coffee.

"Same old crap. I feel like all I do when we get together is talk about this problem, but it never gets better."

"More trouble with your boys?"

"No. Well, yes, sort of. Not so much them," Diana replied. "It's actually their wives this time, and I'm being made to look bad. No surprise there."

"What happened that got you into it with Anne and Molly? I know you've never really liked Molly, but thought you liked Anne."

"Molly, I gave up on. Actually, I've found the perfect food gift for her Christmas present: a jumbo box of roofing nails. She ate the whole regular box at one sitting last year. Anyway, it's so dumb and complicated. I've dealt with the sibling rivalry between Josh and Adam for what seems like forever, and now it's playing out with their wives. I should have seen it coming. What really burns me up is that my grandbabies are getting involved in this now."

"I thought things were calming down between the boys?"

"Apparently not. Essentially I'm being accused of showing more favoritism to Adam's and Molly's kids over Josh's and Anne's kids."

"So what lit this fire?"

"I called Molly to see if I could take Lily to breakfast with Santa downtown. I needed to make reservations because the breakfast fills up quickly. I didn't even think to ask Anne about it because T.J. is too little. I don't think he even understands who Santa is at this point. Anyway, I wanted to do this with Lily as a special day out. Just her and me. At breakfast Santa comes around to each table, sits with the kids. They can have their picture with him, get a little present. Lily is crazy about Santa this year. Well, when Josh and Anne found I had asked Lily and not their little T.J. it was like World War III!"

"How so?" Mary wondered.

"Subtle hints started dropping the last few weeks. I did my best to ignore them. I've found in the past with the boys if I don't rise to the bait the silliness often goes away. I'm not getting into Josh's lifelong grudge about being treated second to Adam. It wasn't true when they were little, and it isn't true now."

"Of course it wasn't."

"Anyway, the subtle hints didn't go away, and now it was Anne making the remarks more than Josh. I expect it of Molly, but not Anne."

"Oh for heavens' sake!"

"Last weekend everyone was over at our house for lunch. Lily was telling Grandpa Jim about her breakfast with Santa. She'd been mesmerized by Santa. Not afraid at all. She told him she wanted new pajamas for Christmas, 'the kind Ariel wore in the movie.' It was darling. Her little face was all lit up with excitement when she was telling him. But across the room, you should have seen Josh and Anne's faces. Their expressions could have stopped a clock."

"They were pouting in front of everyone?"

"Worse than pouting. They glowered. Anne got up from the table and swept her dishes off to the kitchen, muttering as she went. Of course, oh-so-sweet Molly asked out loud 'What's her problem?' Then it all erupted. Anne went ballistic on Molly, Adam got all over Anne's case, and Josh defended his wife. It was a mess.

"Stupid me. I tried to calm them down. That was the worst mistake. Anne accused me of treating not only Josh but also her and T.J. as second-class citizens. She said I obviously favored Lily over T.J., just like I obviously favored Adam over Josh. What really fried me was when she said, 'It's so obvious that other people outside the family comment on the favoritism. And you're always trying to make nice with Molly because she's such a bitch.'"

"Oh, God, what did Molly do?"

"She jumped out of her chair, stalked over to Anne and yelled at her, completely out of control, 'Favorites? Who the hell cares what Diana does anyway? Taking

Lily to meet Santa! Big deal. He was just a big, fat drunk in a Santa suit!'

"I looked over at Lily. Her eyes were so big. She looked back and forth between all of us. She was so confused. Tears running down her face, she looked up at her mother and said, 'It's not so. It's not so. It was really Santa.' Then she just curled up in the corner of the couch and cried and cried. I wanted to go over and hold her, but knew that that would set off new fireworks. It broke my heart. It's one thing for adults to be nasty to one another. That's bad enough. But I hate what it does to my grandbabies."

"Poor Lily. I can't believe even Molly would do that in front of the kids," Mary commented.

Diana went on, "Jim was about to blow a gasket. Finally, before Jim tore into all of them, I just stood up and told them all to go home. I said, 'I love Lily and T.J., but I don't like any of you kids very much right now. I'm furious and ashamed that you would make Lily cry. You haven't even been noticing her. Now go home.'" Diana dabbed at the tears spilling down her face.

"This will blow over by Christmas," Mary said uncertainly.

"It's just terrible. We should be able to enjoy our grandchildren without all the baggage their parents are carrying around. So what do you think?"

"Dear heart, let's face it, Molly's pretty unlikable," Mary began. "She'll go to her grave feeling jealous. Her spite could eat through stainless steel. Anne, on the other hand, may just need a chance to cool off. Give her some time maybe and then invite her to breakfast. I bet she'll come around with a heart-to-heart. It's worth a try for Lily and T.J."

Out of tissues, Diana resorted to her paper napkin. "I sure hope so. I really do."

OUR CHILDREN ARE NOT GOING TO
BE JUST OUR CHILDREN—THEY ARE
GOING TO BE OTHER PEOPLE'S HUS-
BANDS AND WIVES AND THE PARENTS
OF OUR GRANDCHILDREN.

Mary S. Calderone

11

Learn to Embrace Diversity in Your Family

I LOOK AT MY FOUR BOYS, WHO ARE
THE COLORS OF SILT, LOAM, DUST,
AND CLAY, AN INFINITE PALETTE FOR
CHILDREN OF THEIR OWN, AND I
UNDERSTAND THAT TIME ERASES
WHITENESS ALTOGETHER.

Barbara Kingsolver

Paisley, an old friend of ours, told us about her trep-idation when she imagined her mother-in-law's reaction to Paisley's son Peter and girlfriend Victoria's announcement of their engagement.

Paisley and her husband, Philip, were crazy about Victoria, whom they had gotten to know during the two years Peter and Victoria dated during their final years of residency at Cook County General Hospital. The fact that Victoria was African American and they were white didn't faze them either. They had always had the notion from the time their son was in his teens that they would trust his judgment on whom he would date. They reasoned she had to have fine qualities and goodness or Peter wouldn't have been drawn to her. They found Victoria to be one in two hundred million, and they were happy to know her and of Peter's and her decision to marry.

Victoria's parents weren't so enthusiastic at first. They liked Peter all right, but they had had someone else in mind for their daughter from the time she made her first cotillion. Now that they had come to know Peter, they had accepted the union too.

Peter's grandmother Masie, the eighty-seven-year-old imperious matriarch of the family, pillar of Saint Swithun's in the Swamp Church, the Woman's Club, member of several boards, was the last hurdle Victoria and Peter had to surmount.

"Grandmother M," as Peter called her, adored her grandson. She expected him, as the scion of the family, to marry one of his classmates from the Wallace School. Grandmother often expressed the feeling that, "all would be well if everyone weren't so discontented with life and we just accepted 'our place' or lot in life" and other subtle or not so subtle remarks signifying her disapproval of intermarriage between races or social classes.

Despite this, Peter said, "Victoria and I want to include everyone in our lives and that includes Grandmother M." So off they went to get Victoria and Grandmother acquainted and to share the news of their engagement.

Paisley paced the floor for an hour, rehearsing the speech she planned to deliver when her mother-in-law made her much expected phone call once Peter's and Victoria's visit ended. Paisley was deep into her imagined speech when the phone rang, startling her. Her caller identification announced Grandmother M's name and phone number.

"Why didn't you tell me?" were Grandma M's first words.

"Oh, Mother," Paisley sighed.

Grandmother continued, "How could you and Philip have kept this from me?"

"Now, Mother," Paisley broke in, "Victoria is a beautiful accomplished young woman, and we love her. What's more important, Peter is head over heels in love with her, so if you don't want to lose him. . . ," she started to threaten.

Grandmother M cut in, "Paisley," she said in a disgusted huff, "Victoria is Catholic!"

Paisley was so flabbergasted she was silent for a few moments. Then she said weakly, "Don't worry, Mother, ecumenism isn't dead, the world will go on, it will be all right." With that, Paisley hung up, ran to Philip, and collapsed laughing in his bewildered embrace. That was four years ago.

This Pentecost Sunday, Grandmother M was in the first pew of the Cathedral an hour early so that she could witness the christening of Peter and Victoria's first child and her first great-grandchild, Maisie Victoria.

If we live long enough and love our children and grandchildren deeply enough, it's guaranteed that we will be invited to expand our hearts and minds to love as our Creator loves. That invitation could come in the form of our adopted grandchild from another country, the marriage of our grandchild to her beloved from another race or religion or social class. It could be that our grandchild is gay.

Our response could be to stick to our conventions, the way we were brought up, and not bend to new ways. We might even feel that we must uphold our "principles." Early on our family learned a more loving way, when we met such an invitation to love a stranger in our midst or adapt to new ways. If we were to err, we wanted to err on the side of love.

Most of the grandparents we know would agree with these sentiments. We've seen the heartache that comes when parents and grandparents say that it's ludicrous to think that they could ever accept that "foreign grandchild as my own," or that child's spouse from another religion or race, social class, or political party. However, breaking the bond of such traditions and opening up to love allows us to grow and change, make discoveries about differences, and learn how very much we have in common.

There's another thing: It is grandparents who have the most influence if a family is to accept a grandchild who is different in some way—race, religion, or sexual orientation, for example.

What we know for sure is that in order for our human family to grow in dignity and self-worth we need to be cherished and respected by others. We elders have nothing to lose and everything to gain in taking this kind of loving leadership. We gain by strengthening our relationship with our family. We gain by broadening our knowledge about others' customs and approaches to life. It does not mean that we give up our identity; we simply enhance it, give it some spice and dimension we wouldn't otherwise know.

As grandparents, we will profit from remembering that we can select the level of relationship we wish to have with our children and their spouses and, ultimately, with their children, our grandchildren. If we are to enjoy the full wonder of grandparenting, let's hope we can move towards appreciation, respect, and even love.

ARE WE NOT ALL CHILDREN OF ONE PARENT?

Book of Malachi

Learn to Embrace Diversity in Your Family

- If you want to establish good relationships with future daughters- or sons-in-law who will be parents of your grandchildren and who come from backgrounds different from yours (or even ones very similar), here are some helpful things to do:
  - Create a space for them to tell their stories and listen attentively to discover the person talking.
  - Ask them about special moments in their growing up; e.g., favorite foods, holidays, customs, etc.
  - Get to know whether there were painful things they went through and how they or their families coped with them.
  - Deliberately open yourself to new people and celebrations. More cities and towns are celebrating diversity through festivals, workshops, and seminars. Plan to attend.

  These practices will also prove helpful if your children and their spouses adopt children from diverse backgrounds.

LISTEN CAREFULLY TO WHAT YOU HEAR. IN THE MEASURE YOU GIVE YOU SHALL RECEIVE.

Gospel of Mark

Accepting Differences Is Not Always Easy

"Clarissa's doing what?" I nearly shouted over the phone.

"She's taking the kids to spend six weeks with her family in Guadalajara," my son said calmly.

"That's terrible. What are you going to be doing while she's gone? Those kids need their dad."

"Dad, I'll be fine. I'm an engineer and can mix a salad. I can even make an omelet."

My son continued, "Look, Clarissa has to live in the middle of Iowa a zillion miles from home. Tessa and Paul need to get to know their mom's family, too. And it's so expensive to fly them down that they might as well stay for a while. Besides, at their ages they'll come back speaking Spanish like Mexicans."

"Well, I just don't like them being there that long," I countered. "What if they get sick? They're not used to the food."

Pete laughed, which got me even hotter. "Don't worry. Clarissa's been making them burritos with chili, frijoles, and all sorts of dishes—even molé. We figured we'd cauterize their stomachs before they went."

I didn't joke along with him. "You're talking about my grandkids, too," I said.

I heard him sigh. After a long pause, Pete said, "Look, Dad, I'm sorry you don't understand it, but that's something you'll have to deal with. I want the kids to love their Mexican family just as much as they love you. They've got to spend time with them to do that. And, yes, I want them to be real bicultural kids. You're always going on about what it means to have visited Germany and the towns your parents came from. I thought that you of all people would sort of understand. You can either moan about this, or you can be happy for the kids. If you can't wish the kids to have a good time, then maybe I shouldn't put them on the phone to say goodbye."

He had me there, and he knew it. Despite being hacked off at getting blackmailed, I was proud that he stuck to his guns. "Well, okay," I conceded, knowing I was whipped.

The kids got on the phone, both talking at the same time. In a rush they told about which clothes and toys they got to take, how they were going to get to go to their Mexican grandpa's store, and on and on. Their enthusiasm only made me more glum. I listened to their happy chatter, while in my head I had visions of taxi rides through dark, narrow streets, virulent bacteria lurking in vendors' tortillas, and other unknown varieties of dangers waiting to harm my two precious grandkids. Fortunately, I didn't have to speak.

Tessa finally said, "We love you, Grandpa. I'll miss the 'super-dupers' you make." I smiled, thinking about swirling the Concord grape jelly with the crunchy peanut butter that I would spread with a flourish on whole-wheat toast for Tessa and Paul—our ritual breakfast we called "super-duper."

Through the lump in my throat I responded with cheer I didn't feel, "Bye, Angel Pie. You have a great time down there. I love you, too."

Paul got on and suddenly had a shy attack. "Bye, Grandpa!" was all he managed.

"Love you, Little Potato. Be good." My wife, Shirley, handed me a tissue to wipe the tear that was heading down my cheek. I handed her the phone.

Using her polished Spanish, Shirley wished Clarissa well. Even that made me feel more distant from my grandkids. I knew it was dumb, but if it hadn't been for Shirley taking some of her Spanish students—among them my son Pete—to Guadalajara to study the language, I wouldn't have Mexican in-laws who lived so far away in miles and in culture.

When Shirley got off the phone, she said, "Well, you didn't rant and rave as much as I thought. In fact, you behaved so well that I'm going to give you a huge treat."

Out of one of the kitchen drawers, she pulled a long envelope. In the envelope were two airplane tickets. Too stunned to say anything, I just sat there. "I know how jealous you are that the Sanchezes get all that time with Tessa and Paul."

"I'm not jealous. That's silly." She ignored that because even as I said it I knew she was right.

"So, to calm your fears and to really understand what Clarissa's family is like, we're going to Mexico for two weeks. First, Guadalajara, a lovely city, then Mexico City for a couple of days, then Cuernavaca in the mountains, Taxco the wonderful silver city, and maybe Puebla. You have a Spanish-speaking guide— me—who knows the territory. And, lest you forget, it's our anniversary coming up, so this is sort of a second, well third, honeymoon. And I got all of this at really great fares."

What could I say to that?

From the moment Lourdes Sanchez hugged me and gave me her warm smile, I knew we were family. She even showed me how to make her fabulous chili rellenos. Tessa and Paul chatted away in their emerging Spanish and flipped back into English with me.

On the last night in Guadalajara, the Sanchezes gave a party for our going away. Right at the end, Tessa came to sit on one knee and Paul—Pablo—on the other. I felt ready to burst with pride and love of these two. "Grandpa," Tessa whispered in my ear, "I'm glad you and Grandma came to visit. I love you." Then she jumped down and ran to one of her Mexican cousins. Remembering something, she ran back. "Grandpa, I still like super-dupers, but now you can make chili rellenos, too." Yes, now I could, no *problema*.

FATHER-IN-LAW: "DO YOU PREFER
TO BE CALLED "BLACK" OR
"AFRICAN-AMERICAN"?
NEW SON-IN-LAW: "I'D RATHER BE
CALLED YOUR SON-IN-LAW."

Anonymous

For All the World to See

Ellen was making her way down the expressway, wondering why the Memorial Day traffic was even heavier going south to the city, than north to lake country as she had expected it to be. She had been headed north to the family lake home herself, when she received a call on her car phone summoning her back to the city for the imminent arrival of her fourteenth grandchild.

Carolyn and Ralph's first baby wasn't due for two more weeks, but Ellen knew better than to expect on-the-dot delivery. However, she had thought later rather than earlier. They knew that the baby was a boy, but even with that element of surprise removed, all of the other typical emotions were there: anxiety, joy, and anticipation. What will he look like? Will he be all right? Will he be a happy child?

The thought of a happy child took her to the thought of the day when Carolyn and Ralph had come to talk to her and her husband Frank about their plans to be married. Actually, Ralph was asking Frank's permission for Carolyn's hand, which shouldn't have been a surprise either, since Ralph was raised properly from his teen years on by a doting grandmother and three loving aunties.

Ellen and Frank were fond of Ralph. In fact, everyone who met him always remarked on what a kind person he was. But because they were an interracial couple—Ralph an African American and Carolyn almost everything else but—Frank and Ellen did have concerns. One of their main concerns was that elements of society were still not accepting of biracial children.

Already she and Frank were feeling protective of any grandchildren that might appear on the scene. Their talk with Ralph and Carolyn left them feeling reassured that they had the maturity and faith in one another to move on with their plans. And so the engagement was announced, the round of parties and showers attended, and the pre-marital counseling started.

For the sake of greater unity, Ralph made the decision to convert to Carolyn's religion. Ellen believed Ralph probably missed the more lively services at his own church, but he never let on that he did. Frank and Ellen's pastors wasted no time in telling them how fond they had become of Ralph during the weeks leading up to the wedding.

By the time Ellen had maneuvered her way through the freeway traffic, the hospital off ramp was just a few blocks away. Now she began thinking how excited Ralph's family must be. This would be his father's first grandchild, his grandmother's first great-grandbaby, and his aunties would also be ecstatic!

Ellen remembered a scene at Carolyn and Ralph's wedding two years earlier. Ralph's family was visiting with Ellen's relatives, exchanging stories and having a wonderful time. Aunt Phyllis, Ralph's favorite, had turned to Carolyn's most imperious aunt and said, "We were all a bit worried for Ralph. We love him so. But now that we have met the family, we can relax."

Finally, Ellen reached the maternity floor. As the elevator opened, right in front of her were Ralph and Frank—smiling from ear to ear and cooing unabashedly.

In the window of the nursery lay her new grandson for all the world to see.

"I" IS SUCH A SLENDER WORD, A SELFISH WORD. "WE" IS BROADER AND ENCHANTING FOR IT DOUBLES THE OUTLOOK.

Mary Paquette

Raising Grandchildren? You Can Do It!

I WANT TO GIVE MY GRANDCHILD A

FUTURE OF BELONGING.

Barbara Kirkland

Back in the late sixties, I cut my teeth on being a social caseworker in a small, sectarian agency in a metropolitan area. I was assigned a caseload of approximately thirty foster children and their foster parents. At that time in the United States, over two million children under the age of eighteen lived with their grandparents. In about half of these homes, the children's mothers also lived under the same roof as their parents.

The stories I came in contact with nearly broke my heart. Older social workers reminded me that if I'd just read classic stories of children being cared for by elder grandparents or aunts and uncles going back to colonial days I'd get a truer perspective. Older people, they said, have been taking care of children's needs for thousands of years of human existence, while the younger generation provides the sustenance for the community.

But the situation in the late 1960s and early 70s was difficult to accept. Unless grandparents had legal custody of their grandchild, neither could have a sense of stability or reliable continuity. As one of my colleagues warned me, "You'll see a lot of kids in limbo, bouncing back and forth between their recently rehabilitated mother and the grandparents." This meant the kids were often without basic health care and other financial assistance. So we did what we could to get the grandchildren and their grandparents out of bureaucratic limbo.

My coworkers were ahead of the times in many ways. But even we could not have foreseen the massive growth in the number of children who depend in greater measure on their grandparents for their primary care. It is estimated that presently more than seven million grandparents are the primary caregivers of their grandchildren in the United States.

One grandmother told us, "On a cold winter morning, the doorbell rang. I stumbled out of bed, raced down to the front door, and there was a six-week-old baby wrapped in a thin blanket lying on my front stoop! There was a note that said, 'She's your granddaughter, Mom!' What could I do? Her mother lived on the streets and did drugs. I took her in!"

Other grandchildren end up in their grandparents' homes because of the death, incarceration, addiction, or divorce of parents. Some kids, especially adolescents, make their own choice to live with their grandparents.

Many times the stories of grandchildren ending up in their grandparents' home are sad, even tragic. Other stories highlight the positive side, too. The grandparents who raise children that we've talked to report that despite all the difficulties and negative feelings that are bound to happen, the caregiving grandparents feel a new purpose and usefulness in "rescuing" their grandchildren.

One caregiving grandfather told us, "I now know exactly what I have to do every morning when I get up." Another said, "I'm working with my medical people to be as fit as I have to be for the next ten years at least. I've got to be young enough to keep up with these kids, and you know what? I've actually lost weight and have more energy now!"

A grandmother said, "I know I'm needed, I have a new lease on life knowing that I'm Shantay's [her nine-year-old granddaughter] lifeline. And she's mine!"

Another said, "Life was getting kind of dull, you know. Now I'm back in the world of school, stories, birthday parties, basketball, and Sunday school." Then she added, "It's really important, in fact I think it's critical, that if you're going to be successful as a grandparent raising your grandchildren, that you have a lot of support: support from your spouse, your other children, friends and neighbors, and your faith community. I don't know how I could do this job without all of them."

There are those who call grandparents our society's "safety net." That concept can be extended. If our children are, in fact, our hope and future, grandparents are our safe harbor to nurture that hope and guarantee our future.

Raising grandchildren? It may not be easy. The circumstances may be tragic. But, we can do it with support, the wisdom of our experience, prayer, and optimism.

THE MOST WONDERFUL THING I REMEMBER ABOUT MY GRANDPAR-ENTS IS WHAT I COULD SEE IN THEIR EYES WAS A SPECIAL KIND OF LOVE NO ONE ELSE COULD GIVE ME. THIS IS NEVER TO BE TAKEN LIGHTLY.

Eda LeShan

Raising Grandchildren? You Can Do It!

- Name any grandparents you know who are rearing grandchildren. If you have a chance to interview these grandparents, consider what questions you would ask; for example:

  - How is the role of being a grandparent rearing your grandchildren different from raising your children?

  - What have you learned that you could pass on to others?

  - What are the greatest needs you have to support grandparents raising their grandchildren? How can the community help? How can the churches and synagogues help?

- Locate support groups for grandparents raising grandchildren in your community. Attend or contact them to inquire of their offered services and needs.

- List all the experiences and skills that you have right now that would make you a great person or couple to raise your grandchild if necessary. Then list the unique challenges that would face you if you needed to raise your grandkids.

- If you are raising a grandchild, do things that make the absent parent(s) more present. For example:

  - Make a scrapbook of things the grandchild's parents liked to do. Start out the scrapbook with a family tree that includes all members.

  - If the parent(s) have died, plan an annual outing on the parent's birthday, to help celebrate the life of the person(s) who has passed on.

- Establish a living memorial such as a contribution to an arboretum or church or art museum in the name of deceased parents you know.

THERE ARE THINGS YOU GET TO
CELEBRATE, THE SECOND TIME
AROUND, REARING YOUR GRAND-
CHILDREN. AS A GRANDFATHER, I
REALLY GET TO BE INVOLVED IN DAY-
TO-DAY CHILD REARING. THE
WORST PART IS HAVING TO DISCI-
PLINE. AS A GRANDFATHER I DIDN'T
HAVE TO DO THAT. BUT WE'RE THE
PARENTS NOW, NOT THE GRAND-
PARENTS, AND WE HAVE TO CARRY
OUT DISCIPLINE, LIKE IT OR NOT. AS
GRANDPARENTS, WE WERE USUALLY
WISE IF WE JUST STAYED OUT OF IT
AND ENJOYED THEM!

Anonymous Grandfather

Every Day in Gratitude

Page and I, for all appearances, had it all, if success were simply a measure of professional accomplishments, sound fiscal management, healthy children, church and community service, and physical appearance. We had come to a time in our lives when it made sense to simplify. We sold our suburban home, large enough to rear several rambunctious children and their passel of pets, and bought a small, one-story converted cottage nestled on the shoreline of one of Minneapolis's many city lakes.

Simplicity to us meant close walking access to stores, church, neighbors, and cultural sites we were able to visit now that we'd simultaneously cut back on our professional practices. Our retirement nest egg, when analyzed, was modest. But by establishing priorities and simplifying, our retirement was sure to be a comfortable one.

As to our relationship with our children we both agreed with the adage we needed to hold them as you would a bird in hand—squeeze too tight and the child will die; open your palm and not hold them secure, and the child will, like a bird, fly away. So we always felt that the children were not our property. They were their own persons and we would treat them that way.

That meant that when our children married and had their own children, we always respected their marriage and ways of handling our grandchildren even if we would have acted differently. We were always there for support, but we wouldn't intrude or interfere.

Then came the day that all parents fear. I was leaving for work on a chilly, fall morning and Page was cleaning up after breakfast. A young officer came to our door, established our identity, and told us he would take us to the hospital where our children and grandchildren were being cared for. There had been a bad accident. Everyone was under observation.

When we arrived we were given the horrific news that our son-in-law and daughter were dead on arrival, but the grandchildren, Andy and Steve, were in stable condition, under observation. After that everything seemed to blur. A chaplain came to comfort us. We heard nothing she said except that Steve and Andy told the chaplain, "No matter what, we'll always be safe with Grandma and Grandpa."

That terrible first night, two old friends came to stay with us. Our friends had themselves lost their beautiful, talented daughter, Lilly, in a tragic car crash that took her life. Besides the enormous comfort they provided from their own experience of grief, they gave us two pieces of advice that we clung to like drowning sailors clinging to the wreckage. They told us, "Cling to each other through all the stress and storms ahead. Secondly, if Lilly had had children, we would still have a part of her with us."

They did more than comfort us, they helped us resolve an unconscious question and argument for us. Should we take Andy and Steve? Were we too old? We'd just gotten used to pre-retirement and were looking at a more leisurely life. The house is too small. All those nagging issues evaporated in the morning fog.

We brought the boys home with us. We took turns staying with them in their new bedroom. Then one night Steve—the older boy—heard a noise downstairs and woke up terrified. I didn't hear it. Instinctively I knew he was afraid. The terrible accident was happening all over for him. I gently asked him what he heard. Steve shrugged, trying to master his fright. I asked him if we should go downstairs together to investigate. He nodded. I asked him if he was afraid. He said, "Yes." So we explored the house together and made sure everything was intact. Then I took him into the kitchen and made some toast and hot chocolate. I said, "Steve, we have to talk about what really happened. We need to tell the truth and not fantasize. I mean we shouldn't make up stories about what frightens us." That opened the floodgates. He poured out what happened the night his parents were killed and how he and Andy were almost killed. It was a miracle they were still alive.

I told him, "Steve, this didn't happen because of something you did or didn't do." And he began to sob. Then both of us were in each other's arms sobbing. Steve cried his heart out that night, but hasn't cried since then. Andy will remember and cry a little bit now and then, but that night was a resolution for Steve.

We are all in counseling. It's one of the best investments we could make. The boy's counselors are amazed at how well-adjusted they are. Yet we continue to grieve every day. We will for the rest of our days.

We try to put ourselves in their shoes. I think when we're eight or ten years old, parents are one- or two-dimensional, not three dimensions, and because of the stability they've found with us, with their friends, their school and church, they've been able to make it and get on with life. Now, that doesn't mean that adolescence won't have its share of problems. That's why we have to stay as active and healthy as we can so we can meet day-to-day challenges. At least now, I don't have to wonder what I'm going to do each day.

Just in our short time raising Andy and Steve we have learned things we could suggest that would support grandparents who are raising their grandchildren. First and foremost we have depended on our faith community. The church community has supported us. People from church committed baby-sitting time, helped us with grocery shopping, cooking, and even cleaning.

Second, we had to make adjustments in our marriage. The day after we got that horrible call, I called the office and resigned. A burden was lifted off my shoulders.

Third, we keep solid contact with the school. The boys' school is doing a wonderful job of including us and advising and informing us of the boy's emotional and spiritual progress along with keeping track of academic advancement.

Finally, it's important to establish parental roles and discipline. This is the one thing I do find difficult. I wish I didn't have to discipline these boys. Early on we had a frank talk with the boys about what we would be for them. We have to set and enforce the rules. As grandparents we didn't have to do that. But, it's part of the deal.

In the end, there are more blessings than not. We're more fit today and more alert than ever, even in our grief.

There are no guarantees. We may be here for another twenty years, or we may not live to see Steve and Andy graduate from college. We live every day in gratitude.

WHEN WE TRULY SEE WITH THE INNER EYE OF GRIEF, WE HAVE A TINKER'S CHANCE OF LOVING; AND WHAT WE LOVE, WE CHERISH; AND WHAT WE CHERISH WILL TRANSFORM OUR GRIEF INTO GRATITUDE.

Anonymous

Twists and Turns

My days as a grandfather have been a bit unusual, filled with countless twists and turns. Compounding the situation around my granddaughter Sarah's birth, my son died at age eighteen, just two years before she was born. My daughter Caitlyn, Sarah's mom, was a habitual drug abuser. She became pregnant after leaving drug treatment. At the time I was told she was pregnant, she had returned to New York after relapsing.

Also, my relationship with a woman in my life was unraveling due in part to the death of my son and the stress of dealing with unresolved grief. I also felt pressured by her to remarry and possibly have more children. But being a parent had not been a rewarding experience to that point, and I was reluctant, frightened, and selfish about the responsibility of doing it again.

When Sarah, my granddaughter, was born, New York Social Services wanted to place her in a foster home because Caitlyn had admitted to IV drug use in the first trimester of her pregnancy. She told me she did stop using during the second and third trimester. I believe her because her behavior had indeed changed leading up to the time of Sarah's birth. Caitlyn was looking forward to being a mom without really being aware of the responsibilities associated with it. She was twenty-four at the time and was just starting to catch up in the maturation process. My ex-wife and I interceded with the New York authorities and the courts granted my ex-wife guardianship. Caitlyn and Sarah returned to Minneapolis, and Minnesota Social Services approved the home environment for my granddaughter.

About thirty days after her return, my daughter's boyfriend came to Minnesota, and my ex-wife helped them find a place, even though she was the guardian and could have prevented them taking Sarah. My daughter found a job, and her boyfriend took care of Sarah while she was working. I should add that the boyfriend thought he was the father. He was not. Sarah is biracial and he didn't come close to matching that profile.

While all this was taking place, my relationship continued to unravel at the same time my former wife Barbara's marriage was also ending. In the meantime, more tragedy struck. Caitlyn contacted endocarditis, an infection of the heart, and surgery was performed twice. A couple of months later, my daughter died of an embolism.

I immediately thought of adopting Sarah. Barbara initially refused to consider that option, maybe because of the situation in her marriage. Nevertheless, Sarah continued to live with Barbara during this time.

I made a commitment to myself that I would stay involved in Sarah's life, and if it became appropriate, I would pursue her adoption. I didn't get that chance. About a year later Barbara had a change of heart and adopted Sarah by having the man who thought he was the father sign away his parental rights.

Although Barbara has adopted her, I went through a court proceeding that also granted me legal guardianship. I assumed financial responsibility for Sarah. That includes her college fund, her schooling, her health and life insurance, her piano lessons, and much more. I have attempted to provide consistency and boundaries for my granddaughter. I also want her to know about her mother and how some decisions in life can harm you forever. I want her to have self-esteem. I want her to be happy with who she is and have as normal a life as she can for someone in her situation.

I have remarried and my wife Mary has been wonderful with Sarah. Sarah knows she can depend on Mary and me for stability, support, and care. We see Sarah weekly and on holidays. Sometimes she sleeps over and brings a little friend.

Mary and I now have a son. I hope the "big sister" relationship gives her a sense of family and responsibility. The one thing I cannot do is have her think for even a moment that we love her the less. Sarah has lost a lot already. She needs to know she is secure with us.

All of us have heard the saying, "Life goes on." It does, but it takes some funny twists and turns along the way.

GRANDMA WAS A KIND OF FIRST-AID STATION, OR A RED CROSS NURSE, WHO TOOK UP WHERE THE BATTLE ENDED, ACCEPTING US AND OUR LITTLE SOBBING SINS, GATHERING US UP IN HER LAP, RESTORING US TO

HEALTH AND CONFIDENCE BY HER
AMAZING FAITH IN LIFE AND IN A
MORTAL'S STRENGTH TO MEET IT.

Lillian Smith